Puerto Rico

Puerto Rico

Independence, Industrial Policy, and Growth

Luis Gautier

LEXINGTON BOOKS
Lanham • Boulder • New York • London

Published by Lexington Books
An imprint of The Rowman & Littlefield Publishing Group, Inc.
4501 Forbes Boulevard, Suite 200, Lanham, Maryland 20706
www.rowman.com

Unit A, Whitacre Mews, 26-34 Stannary Street, London SE11 4AB

British Library Cataloguing in Publication Information Available

Library of Congress Cataloging-in-Publication Data

Names: Gautier, Luis, author.
Title: Puerto Rico : independence, industrial policy, and growth / Luis Gautier.
Description: Lanham : Lexington Books, [2017] | Includes bibliographical
   references and index.
Identifiers: LCCN 2017049606 (print) | LCCN 2017041242 (ebook) |
   ISBN 9781498556842 (electronic) | ISBN 9781498556835 (cloth : alk. paper)
Subjects: LCSH: Economic development—Puerto Rico. | Industrial policy—
   Puerto Rico. | Puerto Rico—Economic policy. | Puerto Rico—Politics and
   government—1998-
Classification: LCC HC154.5 (print) | LCC HC154.5 .G38 2017 (ebook) |
   DDC 330.97295—dc23
LC record available at https://lccn.loc.gov/2017049606

♾ ™ The paper used in this publication meets the minimum requirements of American National Standard for Information Sciences—Permanence of Paper for Printed Library Materials, ANSI/NISO Z39.48-1992.

Printed in the United States of America

A mi patria, Puerto Rico.

Contents

Acknowledgments

I am truly grateful to the Social Sciences Research Center at the University of Texas at Tyler for financial support, and Mrs. Unisha Maskey for helping with the data collection process and formatting of the manuscript. I would also like to thank Dr. Carmen Concepción, Chair of the Graduate School of Planning at University of Puerto Rico-Río Piedras campus, and all the staff for providing access to their infrastructure and technical support during the summer of 2015. Additionally, the personnel at the Puerto Rico Legislative library, the José M. Lázaro library at the University of Puerto Rico-Río Piedras campus and the library at the Inter-American University—San German campus for providing valuable support and access to key documents and information. I am indebted to Dr. Edwin Irizarry Mora, professor of economics at the University of Puerto Rico-Mayagüez campus, Dr. Francisco Catalá, professor of economics at the University of Puerto Rico-Río Piedras campus and Dr. Efraín O'Neill, professor of engineering at the University of Puerto Rico-Mayagüez campus for valuable discussions, comments and suggestions. I am grateful to an anonymous referee for valuable comments and suggestions.

Preface

This book puts together a series of articles written between the autumn of 2012 and the summer of 2016. These articles arise from my life-long interest in Puerto Rico's economy, particularly as it pertains to the political-economy relationship with the United States (US). As a Puerto Rican born and raised in Puerto Rico, this is a topic very dear to me, particularly with the inexorable economic contraction and the imposition of the Oversight Control Board in the summer of 2016 by the US government. The Oversight Control Board will likely influence economic and social conditions, and policymaking in Puerto Rico for years to come with tremendous implications for the policy debate. This book seeks to contribute to the policy debate as economic conditions evolve.

The literature on Puerto Rico's economy has certainly studied the potential role of political independence for Puerto Rico to achieve sustained growth and development, but this literature has arguably not penetrated sufficiently into the business and political elites in Puerto Rico. It is therefore one of the goals of this book to make the case for independence from an economic policymaking standpoint (i.e., local autonomy for policymaking) with international trade at the center of the analysis. At the same time statehood and the current political status are ruled out (on economic efficiency grounds) as potential paths forward for sustained development and economic growth.

The economy of Puerto Rico presents a unique case study to look into the political-economy analysis of US economic policy in the Caribbean Basin. Since the US invasion in 1898, Puerto Rico has exhibited unique political and economic dynamics, particularly as it pertains to the role of unilaterally set economic policies by the US government. These policies were implemented in Puerto Rico during a period of time where the world economy was not as globalized as today and, more importantly, these policies have not adapted to changing global market conditions. As a result, Puerto Rico's economy has not been able to enjoy the net potential benefits from freer trade-oriented policies. Puerto Rico is experiencing its deepest economic crisis since the early twentieth century, and for Puerto Rico to tackle the current economic debacle it is crucial to re-think development and economic policymaking with global trade at the center of the debate.

When one talks about trade policies in the context of Puerto Rico the political-economy relationship between the United States and Puerto Rico inevitably arises: Puerto Rico is simply not able to set trade policies in the best interest of Puerto Rico's economy because trade policies set by the United States seek to benefit first and foremost the US economy (the US and Puerto Rico economies are very different on an important number of aspects and so policies set on one are not necessarily going to be consistent with the needs of the other). And trade policies set by the United States apply almost entirely to Puerto Rico. This leaves policymakers in Puerto Rico with their hands tied if development policies have international trade as their guiding principle. This policy constraint has reflected more recently since the mid-1990s: an important share of foreign (American) capital has left Puerto Rico (as a result of changing global conditions and the phasing-out of US federal tax incentives, among others) with no real substitute for economic growth and, as a result, local policymakers opted for increased government borrowing to maintain a certain (unsustainable) level of economic activity. Without a real alternative mechanism to stimulate growth, therefore, Puerto Rico's economy won't be able to achieve sustained development and growth.

The aforementioned policy constraint is further exacerbated by the imposition of the Oversight Control Board in 2016 (the Board) on Puerto Rico by the US government. The Board is a *de facto* government which leaves local officials with very little say (or no say at all) on economic and social policy issues. The expectation is that the Board will force Puerto Rico's policymakers to implement severe austerity measures in order to help Puerto Rico regain access to credit markets. However, at the time of this writing the Board has offered very little on effective policies to enhance economic development and growth. The approach thus far has been on the imposition of severe austerity measures.[1]

Even though some of the measures dictated by the Board are indeed positive, measures to promote economic growth via international trade (e.g., reduce trade costs, enhance access to international market) have been, for the most part, absent from the policy mix. This is even as international trade is regarded as a fundamental component for achieving efficiency gains and promoting economic growth and, consequently, helps restore access to capital markets. Unfortunately, potential efficiency gains arising from international trade (i.e., from trade-oriented policies) are not part of the policy debate in

Puerto Rico, and do not seem to be part of the Board's vision to put Puerto Rico back on a path to sustained growth and development.

This book argues that policymaking consistent with trade-oriented policies may serve as an engine for *sustained* growth and development, and aid Puerto Rico regain access to credit markets and tackle its current economic crisis. However, under the current political-economy relationship with the United States, policymakers in Puerto Rico are not able to implement a policy framework such that the net benefits from trade are maximized. As a result, it is really hard to make a strong case for Puerto Rico's economy to recover under either the present colonial political status or statehood on grounds of economic efficiency (see Gamaliel [2016] for a comparative historical analysis of the colonial process in the Caribbean region). That is, I argue that an equilibrium characterized by political independence (i.e., national sovereignty) opens the door to enjoy the net benefits from global trade in a more cost-efficient fashion and, therefore, put Puerto Rico's economy back on a path to *sustained* growth and development. Importantly, I also argue that a freer trade-oriented policy regime is not only in the best interest of Puerto Rico's economy, but also the US economy.

I truly hope the discussion presented in this book signifies an important contribution to the policy debate in order to address Puerto Rico's economic challenges.

January 2017

NOTE

1. See letter from the Oversight Board for Puerto Rico to the Governor of Puerto Rico, dated January 18, 2016, which is available here: https://www.docdroid.net/qQ3aJ1y/oversight-to-rr-jan-18-2017.pdf.html

Chapter 1

Trade and Independence for Economic Development

The potential for sustainable economic growth and development is latent in Puerto Rico's economy. But for factors of production to be used effectively and efficiently, Puerto Rico's economy requires access to markets, particularly to international markets at lower costs. Access to international markets would undoubtedly help, *inter alia*, restore market credibility, regain access to credit markets at bearable costs and achieve important efficiency gains. These are three key elements to help put Puerto Rico's economy back on a path to sustainable growth and development.

But to achieve the sort of market access Puerto Rico requires, Puerto Rico needs to move away from a statehood-like equilibrium and toward political independence, that is, national sovereignty. Without national sovereignty Puerto Rico's policymakers are less likely to have control over trade policy, an absolutely essential policy tool to regain access to global markets at much lower transaction costs. Moreover, control over crucial macroeconomic variables is impossible without national sovereignty.

This book argues, on efficiency grounds, that not only it is in the best interest of the United States (US) to help Puerto Rico move gradually toward an equilibrium consistent with political independence (i.e., national sovereignty), but also that political independence is a sufficient condition to put Puerto Rico back on a growth path via access to global markets at much lower transaction costs. In the analysis the statehood-like equilibrium route is ruled out on efficiency grounds.

The overarching objective of this book is twofold. First, I want to show that industrial policy (e.g., lower taxation, local content requirements) are efficient in an equilibrium consistent with national sovereignty. Second, additional access to global markets at lower costs, an aspect consistent also with national sovereignty, would help get Puerto Rico back on a growth path.

1

Even though aspects of institutional requirements (e.g., types of institutions) are important in the growth literature and in the design of industrial policy, the discussion of the role of institutions goes beyond the scope of this book and it is therefore left as a future line of research. Aspects of industrial policy and general macroeconomic effects are suggested as future lines of research.

Puerto Rico is experiencing its deepest economic crisis since the first half of the twentieth century. The unique political and economic relationship between the United States and Puerto Rico is at the center of the crisis. With these in mind, this book presents policy recommendations for Puerto Rico. A set of partial equilibrium models are employed to study industrial policy and trade issues. The book also discusses the potential role of market-based environmental policies as well as issues of income convergence. The chief result from the analysis is that it is in the best interest of Puerto Rico and the United States to set economic policies consistent with an equilibrium characterized by political independence for Puerto Rico.

International trade ought to be at the center of economic policy reform for Puerto Rico. The basic rationale is that increased access to international markets is likely to yield net benefits to consumers and producers, and promotes a better functioning of markets. The net potential benefits arising from international trade are not presently being maximized and so a re-shaping of policies is needed if Puerto Rico is to experience sustained economic development.

The main thesis of this book is that in order for Puerto Rico's economy to grow in the medium and long term, policies targeted at encouraging international trade are key. Policies to promote trade should be implemented at once in a gradual fashion. It is argued that in order to achieve this goal more local autonomy and less dependence on the US economy (except for perhaps increased freer trade with the United States, but less dependence on the US federal government) are crucial. The analysis relies on economic theory to convey the main point: the fundamental economic mechanism needed for Puerto Rico to get back on a growth path can be accomplished more effectively and efficiently through more autonomy as it pertains to the economic policy arena, particularly trade policy. In other words, because of its geographic characteristics and location, and size of the domestic market, international trade is a crucial component in the island's potential for economic growth. However, net benefits from international trade are not presently being maximized under the current economic framework and, therefore, promoting international trade is key to boost economic growth.

The economy of Puerto Rico is not independent of its politics since in many important ways the particulars of policymaking (e.g., tax credit for foreign corporations) depend largely on the unique political relationship with the United States. This book does not delve into the political debate in Puerto Rico since it has been studied extensively elsewhere (e.g., Bloomfield 1985).

Rather, the analysis touches on political aspects in the context of economic policy reform. It is shown that, in the context of potential sustained economic growth, in the medium and long term statehood offers few inefficient and no clear-cut economic mechanisms to promote growth and that more autonomy in economic policymaking is therefore crucially needed.

The analysis presented in this book is in many ways new to the literature not only because of the formal treatment of many of the issues, but also because of the emphasis on the key message: Puerto Rico needs to increase access to international markets, and in order to achieve this more autonomy in the economic policy arena is imperative. Indeed, the literature on the economy of Puerto Rico has touched on the issue of international trade. For example, Curet (1985, 2003), Banjamín-Torres (1975), Catalá (2013) and Albizu-Campos (1930) and González (1967) just to name a few, argue that in the context of Puerto Rico trade is not sufficiently diversified and too focused on trade with the United States, thereby rendering the local economy almost entirely at the mercy of US economic fluctuations. Moreover, the specialized trade regime with the United States has created a situation where US capital inflows (which promote capital-intensive sectors) crowded out local investment and capital creation and, as a result, the local economy has had no control over wealth creation and thus development. In other words, development depends crucially on foreign US corporations and the policy set unilaterally by the United States (e.g., benchmark interest rate, tax incentives, among others). The crowding out of local investment and lack of control of the local economy (and policy variables) are two key challenges listed also in a report by the US Department of Commerce (1979), Curet (2003) and the Tobin report in 1975. The issue is therefore not new, but a new dimension to it is presented here so as to encourage further research in this area.

The present analysis indicates that without a higher degree of local autonomy (i.e., national sovereignty) for economic policymaking it will be very difficult to maximize the true net benefits from international trade at bearable costs, a key component for growth. Net benefits arise from a more competitive access to international markets which create a more competitive, diversified and dynamic economy. It is furthermore argued that these mechanisms are not possible to be implemented efficiently under statehood, where more political representation and a mild increase in net federal transfers are possible (GAO 2014). In other words, additional representation in the US Congress, the presidential vote, additional net positive transfers and less uncertainty do not translate into the economic mechanisms (e.g., sustained increases in productivity and innovation) needed to maximize net benefits from international trade.

There are several important research questions which this book seeks to answer. First, is it in the best interest of the United States and Puerto Rico to set industrial policies consistent with a higher degree of autonomy for Puerto Rico? If so, what are some potential policies? What is the role of such policies in the Caribbean Basin? Second, does becoming a state of the United States offer efficient economic mechanisms to put Puerto Rico in a sustained growth path? Is there strong evidence to suggest that representation in the US Congress translates into sustained economic growth for Puerto Rico and access to federal funds at a lower cost? Third, in the presence of increasing international competition and access to the US market via bilateral trade agreements, is fiscal independence welfare-enhancing for the United States, Puerto Rico and competitors in the Caribbean Basin? Fourth, what is the potential role of market-based environmental policies in Puerto Rico and to what extent are policymakers in Puerto Rico able to reap the benefits from such policies?

The method of analysis consists of international oligopoly models. The study of industrial policy is consistent with this framework of analysis. More generally, the various theoretical models presented contribute to the literature of industrial policy in the context of the Caribbean Basin. The discussion of environmental policy is new to the literature of Puerto Rico, where basic regression analysis is employed. The method employed to study the economy of Puerto Rico and its role in the Caribbean Basin is new to the literature.

There are three key contributions of this work. The chief contribution is that it analyzes the US-Puerto Rico relationship using formal (mathematical) economic modeling. Even though there are a number of books which analyze the US-Puerto Rico economic and political relationship (e.g., Dietz 2003; Venator-Santiago 2015), none of them do so from a formal economic modeling standpoint. The book, therefore, fills this void in the literature. Additionally, the various theoretical models presented here contribute more generally to the existing literature of industrial policy. A second important contribution is that the analysis emphasizes the discussion of new policy recommendations not only for Puerto Rico in the context of the United States but also the Caribbean Basin. This contribution is relevant to policy discussions particularly in the context of a globalized economy where, increasingly, countries compete to attract foreign investment. Third, the discussion of the potential role of market-based environmental policies in the context of Puerto Rico is entirely new to the literature. The discussion of environmental policy is important given not only the fundamental role of the energy sector in economic development but also the increasing role of international environmental policies in the development of national policy.

The work is structured as follows. Chapter 2 presents a non-technical analysis of the extent to which increased international trade is key for Puerto Rico and how access to global markets may help lead the economy back to a growth path. The key argument is that under the current economic development framework it is too costly for the local economy to maximize the gains from trade, which is a key ingredient for economic growth. Among others, this is because under the current economic development framework trade cost minimization (i.e., the potential to minimize trade costs) and efficiency gains arising from reduced trade barriers and access to world markets are simply not possible to obtain from a practical standpoint. Furthermore, it is argued that under statehood it is prohibitively costly to enjoy the net benefits from more trade openness and, therefore, more autonomy in the economic policy arena is needed.

Chapter 3 presents a theoretical model to argue that further autonomy would enhance welfare in the United States and Puerto Rico, and thus it is in the best interest of both countries to move toward working together as two independent economies, that is, an equilibrium away from either the current commonwealth or statehood political status. The crux of the argument is as follows. First, tax incentives provided by the US federal government have attracted foreign direct investment to Puerto Rico. However, these tax incentives would vanish (or diminish tremendously) under statehood and diminish dramatically in the present political status. Therefore and under relatively general conditions, it can be shown that the ability to attract foreign firms to the local economy via a closer fiscal and political relationship with the United States vanishes. As a result, stronger incentives can be offered by the local economy in an equilibrium where the two economies work independently, thereby raising welfare in each of the two economies. A similar argument is put forward by Negrón-Rivera (1997), albeit in a less rigorous analytical framework. The analysis calls for a gradual transition toward fiscal independence, an equilibrium consistent with political independence.

Chapter 4 explores issues of increased regional competition as a result of increased bilateral trade agreements between the United States and countries in Latin America and the Caribbean. Several policy reforms and their effect on production decisions are explored. The idea here is that with increased international competition Puerto Rico no longer has unique access to the US market, a scenario with repercussions for Puerto Rico's economy (and policy-making in Puerto Rico) as well as many of the economies in the Caribbean Basin. To put the analysis into context the case of the Dominican Republic (and CAFTA-DR) is used, where US unilateral policies and trade agreements with the Dominican Republic (DR) have increased access to the US market to firms (US firms) operating in the DR. The analysis suggests that a unilateral reduction (by the United States, say) in taxes faced by firms operating in the region results in gains to all parties involved; even though subsidies may yield similar results, subsidy payments may create budgetary pressures. Additionally, a higher degree of product differentiation may ameliorate the cross effects of policy thus suggesting a potential policy reform for countries facing intense competition. In the context of Puerto Rico, the analysis suggests that higher taxes result in higher output of firms operating in Puerto Rico only if subsidy payments compensate the increase in taxation. This result suggests that for foreign firms operating in Puerto Rico to experience more production (to cater the US market) additional subsidy payments (or tax credits) are needed. Therefore, results suggest that a low-tax equilibrium is likely to benefit the country setting the policy unilaterally (i.e., United States). This is a scenario consistent with an equilibrium away from statehood and the present colonial status.

Chapter 5 explores political-economic aspects of policy setting. In particular, a model of lobbying is employed to show that a low-tax equilibrium is likely to take place as foreign (US) firms lobby for lower taxation. It is also shown that attempts by the Puerto Rican government to boost job creation by commanding foreign firms to employ local resources moves the equilibrium closer to a lower tax. As argued in chapter 3, lower taxation is associated with an outcome which takes the economy away from a statehood-like equilibrium unless more aid comes from the US government in the form of subsidies or tax credits. I argue that this aid is unlikely to take place at the present time, particularly in the presence of the Oversight Control Board established in 2016 by the US Congress.[1]

Chapter 6 relies on the existing theoretical literature on the local content requirement to make the case that for some industries it makes sense for Puerto Rico to set a local content requirement. The ability to implement such policies depends on the degree of autonomy of policymakers in Puerto Rico, for example, local content requirement rules depend almost entirely on US government ruling. Thus, the potential gains from the implementation of local content requirements are consistent only with a non-statehood-like equilibrium.

Chapter 7 presents a brief analysis on income converge. The key message from this chapter is that there is no strong evidence for converge with the US economy, thereby raising questions about whether Puerto Rico's economy, as a state of the United States, would experience income convergence with the US economy. It is also argued that the empirical literature does not provide strong evidence to suggest that additional political representation in the US government for Puerto Rico is likely to translate into sustained growth.

Chapter 8 deviates a bit from trade issues and presents a brief analysis of how environmental policy may help address environmental and economic issues in the local (Puerto Rican) economy. The analysis is relevant and fits within the scope of this book because (i) it proposes a way forward to address current infrastructure, pollution and revenue challenges for the Puerto Rico's Electric Power Authority—electricity markets are a fundamental component to promote growth— and (ii) it underlines the need for national sovereignty to achieve much-needed market efficiency gains. It is argued that environmental policy is a policy area which Puerto Rico has not exploited, but which should be given more attention in the policy debate. The analysis argues for market-based environmental policies in order to promote innovation, raise government revenue and address damages from pollution, among others. A brief review of local efforts to address environmental issues is presented. Even though federal regulation poses few limitations in the US-Puerto Rico context, it may pose substantial limitations in an international context to provide local policymakers the authority to potentially establish cross-country (e.g., Caribbean Basin) pollution permit regimes and environmental targets via cross-country agreements. Welfare gains via cross-country agreements are unlikely to be achieved without a higher degree of autonomy (i.e., national sovereignty) in the economic policy arena. The role of environmental policy in an international context is becoming increasingly important as the challenges from climate change are addressed by the international community. Puerto Rico could potentially take the lead in environmental policymaking in the Caribbean Basin and enjoy the benefits of a regional energy market in the presence of region-wide market-based environmental policies.

The analysis presented in this book does not seek to be exhaustive in terms of analyzing the myriad of factors which characterize Puerto Rico's economy. Rather, the book seeks to present key topics about Puerto Rico's economy, derive policy recommendations and motivate further research. For instance, the analysis in chapter 8 may serve as an initial literature review and could be used to conduct more detailed statistical analyses about the potential role of market-based environmental policies in Puerto Rico, an area of research which has not been explored in detail. Additionally, the analyses in chapters, 3, 4, 6 and 8 could be extended to a general equilibrium setting and present estimations of gains/losses for the local economy as a result of increased global trade. The theoretical analysis relies on partial equilibrium models and so a natural extension would be to explore a general equilibrium setting and, moreover, test some of the hypotheses empirically.

Furthermore, a more detailed analysis of the role of US transfers to Puerto Rico is warranted. Even though chapter 4 explores the important role of transfers in the context of subsidy payments, an important contribution to the literature would be to analyze the role of transfers in the Puerto Rican economy from a theoretical standpoint, for example, Pantojas-García (2007) and Blanco-Peck (2009) analyze the role of transfer payments in Puerto Rico's economy and electoral outcomes, albeit not in a formal economic modeling framework. Additionally, empirical analyses to estimate the effects (net benefits) of a gradual transition to a more open-economy policy regime are needed. This would provide policymakers with a sense of the time path of the economy as Puerto Rico transitions gradually away from a statehood- or colony-like equilibrium. In a historical context descriptive analyses have been presented (e.g., Duprey-Delgado 2016) as to the extent of a potential framework for a gradual transition; however, a more quantitatively oriented approach may certainly complement existing analyses.

NOTE

1. Public Law No: 114–187, June 30, 2016. The reader is referred to the Natural Resource House Committee for more information: http://naturalresources.house.gov/issues/issue/?IssueID=118691

Chapter 2

Market Potential and International Trade

There are numerous factors which may help explain the current economic crisis in Puerto Rico. Potential policy recommendations have been put forward by the government, the private sector, non-profit organizations as well as the public at large. However, the literature on Puerto Rico's economy has discussed the potential for growth and policy recommendations only to some extent, thereby leaving room for additional policy recommendations, particularly from an international trade standpoint.[1] Therefore, the main objective of this chapter is to briefly describe the current economic crisis in Puerto Rico and offer additional policy recommendations. I argue that international trade should be at the center of economic development for Puerto Rico and that policymaking should evolve around encouraging trade. The idea here is that additional access to international markets is likely to encourage job creation, reduce the price of goods and services consumers face and the cost of inputs to producers, and expand consumer choice. These are all important positive effects on the economy which can be argued on efficiency grounds.

There is an extensive empirical literature which points to the positive connection between trade openness and income growth, thereby substantiating the analysis of the potential role of trade to enhance growth in the case of Puerto Rico, for example, Dollar (1992), Sachs and Warner (1995), Frankel and Romer (1999), and Wacziarg and Welch (2008). In the context of Puerto Rico, moreover, Vega-Rosado (2006) argues, using Porter's model of competitiveness, that Puerto Rico has lost ground in terms of global competitiveness on several industries, but also identifies export areas where competitiveness can be improved (e.g., health sector, pharmaceuticals and food processing). These results further substantiate the analysis of the role of trade to enhance growth.[2]

The economy of Puerto Rico has been characterized historically by having the United States (US) as its principal trading partner. At the same time there is evidence which indicates the presence of important trade restrictions (non-trade barriers and import tariffs in some sectors) in the United States (e.g., Egger et al. 2015; Jouanjean, Maur and Shepherd 2015; UNCTAD 2012) thus suggesting potential areas for larger gains from trade to Puerto Rico's economy. This is because US trade regulation applies almost entirely to Puerto Rico's trade legal framework. In other words, there exists the potential for Puerto Rico to grow its economy via a higher degree of freer trade by reducing the trade restrictions currently present in the US regulatory framework. In what follows I discuss this in the context of international trade and what I call "market potential."

Puerto Rico's economy has not been able to deliver the rate of growth one would expect to enhance economic development.[3] The rate of growth of real GDP exhibits a rapid decrease since 2001, and the number of total nonfarm employment, particularly in the manufacturing sector, has decreased dramatically since 2006 (see figures C.1 and C.2). Additionally, bank deposits have diminished and the government is currently facing a fiscal crisis, which has impacted the ability to borrow at bearable costs and therefore invest in much needed infrastructure projects, human capital, among others. The current macroeconomic situation is, consequently, likely to take a toll on social problems such as crime and poverty. A discussion about policy options to tackle the crisis seems relevant.

In a recent article published in the newspaper *Diálogo*, Dr. Juan Lara puts the current economic situation in a historical context and argues that the development model employed in Puerto Rico was consistent with a period of time where the global economy experienced a slowdown in the volume of trade, shrinking globalization and rising protectionism.[4] However, after the Second World War the global economy experienced a decrease in protectionism (i.e., tariff reduction) and, as a result and among other factors, the volume of global trade increased. The economic development model used in Puerto Rico has not evolved since to adapt to a more globalized world; it was a model designed to reap the benefits from a non-globalized world economy. I agree with Dr. Lara's view on the current economic crisis in Puerto Rico: it is indeed a symptom arising from an economic model which has not been able to adapt to a more globalized world. As a result, the discussion of policy options in the context of international trade seems relevant.

According to many government officials, academics and people in the private sector, it is possible to take the necessary steps to address the economic problems Puerto Rico faces. Some of the proposals include a smaller government to deal with the short-run fiscal challenges and reduce its crowding-out effect on private investment. And others contend that a diversified, export-oriented economy should be at the center of the economic model to promote economic activity in the medium and long term. Lowering energy costs has been also mentioned as a key to create an adequate investment environment and benefit consumers via lower energy prices. Others argue that Puerto Rico should (i) allocate resources to make sure that local entrepreneurship plays a prominent role in the manufacturing sector and (ii) promote the agricultural sector and tourism sectors in a coherent fashion. Even though these do not represent an exhaustive list of policy recommendations, they exemplify some of the policy options Puerto Rico has available to tackle the crisis and which have been consistently part of the policy debate (for examples of policy options the reader is referred to Dietz (2003), Lara (2014), Collado-Schwarz (2012), Marques-Velasco (1993), Catalá (2010; 2013), Lawrence and Lara (2006), Krueger, Teja and Wolfe (2015)). I do not necessarily disagree with these policy recommendations. Indeed, I believe Puerto Rico needs to give some of these a hard look and move forward with their implementation sooner rather than later.

But in the context of policymaking, it might help formulate and implement some of these policies by thinking about them as part of an overarching policy objective, *viz.*, the creation of *market potential* for Puerto Rico's economy. What do I mean by the creation of *market potential*? In a nutshell, this means that Puerto Rico needs to find sufficient opportunities to buy and sell goods and services in a sustainable and efficient fashion in order to boost economic development. Access to international markets is the linchpin of *market potential*. The larger this market potential the better the chance, for example, for local and foreign businesses to make profits and re-invest in the local economy, and create high-salary paying jobs for the local labor market. Indeed, Dietz (2003, 135) indicates that Puerto Rico's economy has not reached its potential for economic growth given the factors of production available in the country: "Growth rates have been lower than would be expected given Puerto Rico's inputs to production." Thus, policies which have been already suggested should be looked through the lens of what I call *market potential*. Examining policies through this lens provides a clear target, which should in turn guide the development of a consistent policy framework in a coherent fashion.

To see this, consider the current short-run fiscal challenges. Even though there are different views about how to deal with it (e.g., via reductions in government spending and/or tax increases), it is clear that the room the government has to maneuver is very small. That is, there are large fiscal constraints to implement appropriate policies adequately. In particular, the government in Puerto Rico does not have the ability to borrow from international institutions such as the International Monetary Fund, the Word Bank (e.g., International Financial Corporation at www.ifc.org), among others. In this context the market potential for the government to borrow is limited and no policies to increase this market potential seem to be at the center of the policy debate. Notice that this is not necessarily a line of reasoning to argue in favor for more borrowing. Rather, it is simply a rationale which I believe should be seriously considered. This is because by having additional sources to borrow from in the short-run Puerto Rico may be able to be in a better position to reduce its borrowing costs. Or at the very least have access to credit markets at arguably reasonable costs in order to make sure that it is capable of borrowing what it really needs, at bearable borrowing costs, to address the short-term fiscal issues and, at the same time, implement credible policies gradually so that the economy is able to follow a path to recovery. Again, the idea here is not to debate about the benefits and costs of Keynesian policies and the role of government,[5] but rather to acknowledge that there might be a real potential to lower borrowing costs to address short-run fiscal issues by enhancing the access to markets.[6]

The notion of market potential is also applicable to the private sector. It is probably fair to say that, in general, businesses do not regard as favorable high labor and energy costs, and excessive regulation. Even when these may be factors which do not play favorably for an "adequate" business environment, it is also true that the current market potential (i.e., access to international markets) for businesses in Puerto Rico is limited; access to international markets would help offset those factors conducive to an unfavorable business environment. Without policies designed to make sure that businesses reach their market potential, it will be very costly to expand local production sufficiently so that the local economy can create a sufficiently large number of jobs. If it had been possible, it would have probably occurred already under the current institutional framework. To see this, suppose that Puerto Rico is able to create a favorable and adequate business environment. Does this mean that the private sector will create sufficient jobs so that the labor participation and unemployment rates see substantial and sustained improvements and reductions, respectively? Does this mean that economy-wide incomes will rise and investment levels catch up with those present in high income countries? The answers to these questions are debatable. But what one can assert is that, in the current political and economic policy institutional framework, businesses operating in Puerto Rico cannot reach their market potential. In particular, as part of the trade and customs union of the United States, Puerto Rico has, on the one hand, free access to the US market (an important market indeed), but on the other it is not able to reap the potential net benefits from rapid growing markets, partly because of the current trade regulatory framework in the United States, which applies directly to Puerto Rico's economy. That is, in the current institutional scenario reaching the market potential for businesses is prohibitively costly, not because it does have access to the US market, but because it does not have access to rapid growing markets at a reasonable cost. This is the opportunity cost of being part of the US custom and trade union, which is particularly relevant to Puerto Rico given its geographical characteristics and size of its domestic market.

Thus, what can be done about this? To answer this question it is important to have a sense of the trade barriers the United States currently has in place and for which sectors. These trade barriers offer a sense of the forgone market potential for Puerto Rico's economy. For instance, the United States imposes relatively high tariff barriers not only on sectors related to foodstuffs (Bown and Crowley 2016), but also in sectors such as "processed foods," "primary agriculture" and "other manufacturers" (see figure 3, Egger et al. 2015). Specific examples include potential tariffs on solar panels made in China between 24 percent and 36 percent (Lawrence and Datla 2013) as well as a 16 percent tariff on jeans made with cotton produced in China (Delpillis 2013). There are also a number of important non-tariff barriers (e.g., countervailing and antidumping duties, safeguards, labeling), which the United States has imposed overtime on a number of goods (e.g., semiconductors from Korea, labeling of "dolphin safe" on tuna coming from Mexico and a number of food products exported into the United States). Indeed, non-tariff barriers have not only in the past played an important role in trade policy and potentially the flow of trade (e.g., Walter 1969; Nogués, Olechowski and Winters 1986), but also presently in the negotiation of new trade agreements, particularly in a global trade regime which has experienced a reduction in import tariffs (e.g., UNCTAD 2005, 2007, 2012; Chin, Rusli and Khusyairi 2015; Eggers et al. 2015; Vinokurov et al. 2016). These tariff and non-tariff barriers illustrate forgone welfare gains for Puerto Rico's economy via trade.

The case of potential trade restrictions on Chinese solar panels is an interesting one because it illustrates the case where a trade policy has been imposed in the interest of US industry, not Puerto Rico. Without trade barriers (or threats about potential trade barriers) Puerto Rico could have potentially benefited from lower prices on solar panels. It is noteworthy that, although unlikely, trade barriers may trigger further trade restrictions between the United States and its trading partners, which represent, again, trade restrictions detrimental for Puerto Rico's economic development. There are many other examples where the United States has (or may) impose trade restrictions to Chinese producers (e.g., steel rod, solar panels, crawfish meat tails, tires for certain vehicles, thermal paper, polyethylene terephthalate film), Mexican producers (e.g., cement production and large residential washers), India and Turkey (e.g., oil country tubular goods used by the natural gas industries) and Korean (e.g., large residential washers). Again, these are potential gains from trade that Puerto Rico could benefit from, if it could eliminate or avoid such trade barriers.

In addition, there are a number of trade barriers between the United States and the European Union (EU) which arguably increases trade costs to EU companies exporting to the United States. Examples of industries facing trade barriers (tariff barriers) include leather goods, textiles, footwear, railway cars; and non-trade barriers (e.g., regulatory) include automobile, pharmaceutical, textiles, cosmetics, and wine and spirits, among others (EC 2009). More recently, in a 2015 report the European Commission (EC) states that there are trade restrictions imposed by the United States which are of concern to the European Union, including beef, goat meat, egg products and dairy products among other animal products (EC 2015).

Indeed, in a recent report by the USITC (USITC publication 4440), estimates indicate that liberalizing trade in the United States would result in an increase in economic welfare by $1.1 billion. This result indicates that, as part of the US customs union, Puerto Rico could potentially benefit from trade liberalization. In particular, removing trade barriers in the production of cheese, canned tuna, textiles and apparel, and the manufacturing of ceramic and glass products, sugar, and footwear and leather, services (banking sector), among others, may very likely benefit Puerto Rico's economy. From the same report, one can conclude that liberalization may yield large benefits to the overall economy even as the average tariff shows a downward trend.

Furthermore, Egger et al. (2015) estimate the effects of trade liberalization (tariff and reduction and potential reduction in non-tariff barriers) between the European Union and United States. The authors argue that such a trade regime would be on balance beneficial to both economies. This, in turn, suggests that there is room to reduce trade barriers from Puerto Rico economy's standpoint (since the trade regulatory framework in the United States applies directly to Puerto Rico) and, therefore, achieve potential gains from trade in a more liberalized trade regime. Moreover, aspects of environmental regulation, data protection and financial regulation (all areas where non-tariff barriers arguably play an important role) could be dealt with (and with potential welfare gains) on a regional basis should Puerto Rico set its own regulatory framework.

More specifically in the context of Puerto Rico, Lawrence and Lara (2006) discuss potential benefits from public policies targeted at promoting the external sector of the economy of Puerto Rico and the importance of this sector for economic growth. They argue that policies should target sectors which are experiencing market failures in order to use resources efficiently. Indeed, liberalizing trade gradually may well aid in the implementation of such policies, which suggests that by opening the economy to a more liberal trade model current industries may not be, on balance, negatively impacted.

Relatively high tariffs in the case of a small open economy, *ceteris paribus*, are likely to raise the price consumers pay for goods and services (e.g., food and beverages is a key sector to Puerto Rico given that it imports a large proportion), and at the same time they do not create, in a sustainable fashion, the number of jobs Puerto Rico needs in order to boost its economy. Again, had it been possible to create a large number of jobs in a sustainable fashion through trade under the current institutional and regulatory framework, we should have already seen substantial job growth as a result of trade. Thus, what this illustrates is that the current trade policy framework brings relatively higher trade costs to Puerto Rico's economy, thereby creating an unfavorable environment for businesses (export-oriented businesses, in particular) and consumers in Puerto Rico. Higher trade costs are also likely to restrict the entry of a diverse number of foreign capital, an important component for growth.

With this scenario in mind, policies should be targeted at reducing trade costs. Lower trade costs would result in an increase in the volume of trade and therefore more market opportunities (potential) for local businesses. Some of these cost-reducing policies may include the ability to lower tariffs in areas where local businesses may benefit the most, for example, elimination of the tariffs on solar panels built in China may help boost renewable energy in Puerto Rico, thereby potentially lowering energy costs, and tariff reductions in the processed food sector. In addition, consumers and businesses may face lower prices if protectionist policies in the food industry imposed by the United States (mainly for the benefit of US producers) are eliminated. For example, protectionist policies in the sugar industry render sugar relatively more expensive for US consumers.[7] The same logic applies to other food items such as dairy products (e.g., milk), corn, soybeans and wheat (Mercier 2011; Bown and Crowley 2016). Liberalizing trade in food-related sectors is key in the case of Puerto Rico due to its geographical location and factor endowments. The fishing industry in Puerto Rico is an example of an industry within the food-related sector where US regulation (i.e., cross-country agreements) does not allow Puerto Rico to benefit fully via income through fishing permits or the development of local capital (Pizzini 2011).[8]

Furthermore, the United States currently faces trade barriers to export some of its goods and services abroad; in fact, there is evidence which suggests that non-tariff barriers have been increasing for US exports in recent years (USTR 2015, 2). By eliminating these barriers Puerto Rico would likely increase trade opportunities and therefore enhance market potential. For example, according to a 2013 report published by the Office of the United States Trade Representative, the Dominican Republic, though a member of the new CAFTA-DR trade agreement which will result in a duty-free market for US products, imposes non-tariff measures on US goods such as medical devices, vehicles and cleaning products. These non-tariff trade barriers pose an opportunity for Puerto Rico, only if it were possible to engage in trade negotiations and establish a completely *de facto* free-trade zone between

Puerto Rico and the Dominican Republic. Another example is the potential to actively engage in trade agreements with members of MERCOSUR (i.e., Brazil, Argentina, Paraguay and Venezuela) and the Caribbean Basin; trade agreements with these blocks of countries are potentially beneficial to Puerto Rico. Additionally, Canada imposes trade controls through province-run liquor control boards of wine and spirits coming from the United States. This is another area where Puerto Rico may increase its volume of trade, that is, another way Puerto Rico may enhance its market potential. It is noteworthy that non-tariff barriers is an important factor which can affect trade flows, particularly as tariffs show a downward trend, see for example, UNCTAD (2005, 2007, 2012) and Nogués, Olechowski and Winters (1986).

Access to the EU market of pharmaceutical products is limited (by numerous reasons) to US exports on several member states such as Austria, Belgium, Finland, France, Hungary, Czech Republic, Italy, Spain and Lithuania and Poland (NTE 2013). This is a key example given Puerto Rico's background on the pharmaceutical industry: having the ability to negotiate with this block may represent a tremendous market potential for the private sector in Puerto Rico. Current numerous investment barriers on US foreign investment are also a potential opportunity which Puerto Rico is missing to boost exports and investment. With the ability to negotiate trade agreements, local businesses can make sure to establish the terms of trade which maximize their net benefits.

In addition to all the aforementioned examples of restrictions to enhance market potential via trade, a key constraint for boosting international trade for Puerto Rico is the US cabotage laws (the Jones Act). These laws raise the cost of trade, thereby representing a large impediment to achieving the market potential needed to create jobs, attract investment and boost exports. In particular, abolishing the cabotage laws would not only reduce the cost of durable and non-durable goods, but also the cost of intermediary goods thereby making local businesses more competitive. The studies by González (1967), Herrero-Rodríguez, Soriano-Miranda and Mari (2001), and Blanco-Peck (2009), for example, suggest that there is strong evidence of higher costs to local businesses arising from the cabotage laws. These laws are therefore a detriment to the prosperity and economic growth of Puerto Rico via international trade, one of the pillars for economic development.[9] Even though the government of Puerto Rico partially offsets trade costs via tax breaks (as well as US federal aid) , the actual cost of engaging in trade, via the caboatge law, is reflected in the inadequate use of government resources to offset the law's effect on trade costs. It is extremely hard to make a strong case to keep the cabotage laws in the context of the Puerto Rican economy, if growth is to be achieved via international trade and resource allocation via markets.

Is the trade restriction via the cabotage laws offset by the current political and economic relationship between Puerto Rico and the United States? The current relationship may only partially offset the negative effects of the cabotage laws via transfer payments and access to the US market. The rapid decrease in Puerto Rico's economic activity over at least the last 10 years (and large loses in total employment in manufacturing since the 1990s) and a small degree of diversification in the economy do not seem to provide a strong case for the thesis that the current US-Puerto Rico relationship benefits Puerto Rico's economy, specifically from a trade-induced growth standpoint. Additionally, the bulk of economic activity has come from foreign (American) corporations and not local ones, thereby suggesting that the access to the US market has not been sufficiently strong to boost growth and job creation so as to substitute the role in the economy of foreign corporations.[10]

Would becoming a state of the United States likely improve the macroeconomic conditions for Puerto Rico and enhance market potential for Puerto Rico? It is hard to make the case for sustained economic growth under statehood since the economic mechanisms whereby the economy would grow, particularly via international trade, are not clear-cut (see Negrón-Rivera (1997) for an analysis of tax-related incentives under statehood, independence and commonwealth, and Blanco-Peck (2009) for an analysis of the connection between dependency of federal funds and Puerto Rico's economy). Indeed, there is nothing which prevents Puerto Rico from establishing a free-trade zone with the United States under independence for Puerto Rico, while making sure it yields large net benefits to Puerto Rico via international trade. As a state of the Union Puerto Rican consumers and producers would face additional costs associated with higher federal income taxes and broader costs to the Puerto Rican economy (GAO 2014). These higher costs (net of federal aid) do not seem to yield the benefits necessary to put the economy in a path to recovery via trade. Moreover, Lara (2014) argues that statehood would not yield an unambiguous improvement in competitiveness and income convergence.[11] Hence, sustained growth via trade does not seem to be consistent with a statehood-like equilibrium.

Carro (2011) describes the legal background under which Puerto Rico's economy currently operates. One of the key messages from the author is that Puerto Rico has the possibility of benefitting from the increase in the number of free trade agreements established by the United States and countries around the globe (e.g., CAFTA-DR, US-Korea). However, what the analysis does not point out very clearly is the foregone benefits from free trade Puerto Rico is currently not enjoying by not being able to implement its own trade policies. This is a potentially large market opportunity which Puerto Rico is currently missing to boost economic development via international trade. Additionally, the increase in trade agreements between the United States and other economies has not been able to offset the economic crisis Puerto Rico has experienced over the last decade. It is important to note that the argument made here is not about choosing between, on the one hand, free trade with the United States and, on the other, free trade with the rest of the world. Rather, the argument is for trade agreements with all potentially beneficial markets to Puerto Rico's economy; this would require the ability of policymakers in Puerto Rico to freely implement trade policy to Puerto Rico's benefit.

Labor markets represent an additional area where Puerto Rico may benefit and reach market potential. For example, those who believe in fewer regulations and lower wages to boost job growth and investment may see a tremendous potential outside the current institutional framework. In particular, the federal minimum wage could be abolished and set in a way so that it fits Puerto Rico's market conditions (Krueger, Teja and Wolfe 2015). Concomitantly, requirements to foreign investment could be implemented (e.g., local content requirements) to boost local businesses and taxes on foreign corporations need not be limited by an upper bound.[12] Federal payroll taxes could be adapted to business conditions in Puerto Rico. In addition, there are markets which could potentially yield business opportunities, new tax revenue and the reduction of the underground economy like, for example, the legalization of illegal drugs. These possibilities could potentially help achieve relatively large short-run gains through the creation of new businesses and a larger tax base. The potential inward flow of foreign capital via freer trade could increase labor productivity and wages, and increase the labor participation rate, thereby improving labor market conditions. A gradual transition toward freer trade could help ensure the reallocation of resources while at the same time cushion potential negative effects on the labor market.

The economy of Puerto Rico over the last decade has not recovered and there is no clear recovery projected in the medium term. In other words, the backbone of the development and economic growth process in Puerto Rico is no longer present, and additional federal funds and more access to the US political arena are not going to either take Puerto Rico back to its growth path via trade, increase productivity levels, or offset the current economic downturn (see chapter 7 for a discussion). Had it been possible, one would have expected to see signs of recovery after more than 10 years of recession. The current crisis is thus quite complex and it will probably take a substantial re-shaping of the regulatory framework to tackle it, particularly regulation directly related to international trade policy.

This chapter concludes by stressing the need for more access to international markets, particularly in the foodstuffs industry, and also suggesting an additional channel whereby access to global markets can enhance economic activity in Puerto Rico. First, the relatively high levels of trade barriers imposed by the United States on the foodstuffs industry not only raises prices to consumers in Puerto Rico, but it effectively closes the door to Puerto Rico to enjoy potentially lower prices in global markets. With a relatively low income per-capita, high food prices curtail the ability of Puerto Rican consumers to spend on other goods and services and/or increase household savings. Second, Puerto Rico could benefit from greater access to global markets by playing a more active role in global supply chains. With relatively lower trade barriers for intermediate goods vis-à-vis final goods across countries (Bown and Crowley 2016), plus Puerto Rico's track record in the manufacturing sector, Puerto Rico could play a leading role in the region.

The last decade illustrates a period of time where the United States and Puerto Rico's economy have shown large differences between their growth rates. Thus, it is important for Puerto Rico to have the flexibility to implement policies based on Puerto Rico's needs, particularly when it comes to trade-induced growth. Clearly, the unique US-Puerto Rico relationship has not been sufficient to achieve sustainable development and economic growth. It is therefore time to look at policy options from a different angle with international trade at the center of the debate.

NOTES

1. For a description of trade statistics the reader is refereed to Irizarry-Mora (2011), Dietz (2003), and the yearly *Economic Report to the Governor* put together by the Puerto Rico Planning Board (http://www.jp.gobierno.pr/).

2. Available: http://eleduca.com/gonzalo/Documentos/Puerto%20Rico.pdf

3. Fuentes-Ramírez (2014) estimates the Human Development Index for Puerto Rico. The author argues that there is a gap between potential and actual human development as a result of income inequality. This result indicates the need for further development in Puerto Rico, which is consistent with what I argue.

4. Among others, Catalá (2008), Curet (2003), Finn (1985) and Pantojas (2010) also talk about the unique historical context in which Puerto Rico's economic policy was implemented.

5. For a discussion on the role of austerity measures the reader is referred to the special issue on "Assessing Austerity" in the *Cambridge Journal of Regions, Economy and Society*. Available http://oxfordjournals.org/our_journals/cjres/assessing-austerity.html

6. Additionally, access to international development programs could help development prospects. Participation in development programs funded by international financial institutions would allow the Puerto Rican economy to boost economic development in targeted, relevant areas (e.g., housing, access to credit for small businesses). Currently, Puerto Rico is not eligible for such aid programs, although it receives funds for similar programs from the US federal government.

7. See Krugman and Obstfeld (2009, 195–196) and http://sugarcane.org/global-policies/policies-in-the- united-states/sugar-in-the-united-states

8. See Pizzini (2011) available http://seagrantpr.org/wp-content/uploads/2014/11/Mirada_al_mundo_de_los_pescadores.pdf

9. There is a strong empirical literature which points to the positive connection between trade and growth and development, for example, Dollar and Kraay (2004), Wacziarg and Welch (2008).

10. There is an important literature on Puerto Rico's economy which indicates that the development of local businesses (i.e., avoid the crowding-out of local businesses as a result of American companies) as well as the diversification of the export market (trade depends too much on the US market and behavior of US foreign corporations) is the key for growth, for example, Curet (1986, 2003), Clark (1930), Finn (1985), Rivera-Ortiz et al. (1990), Benjamín-Torres (1975), Vega-Rosado (2006), just to name a few.

11. See Lara (2014, 12): "Un análisis cualitativo de los determinantes de la competitividad lleva, por lo tanto, a la conclusión de que la estadidad no solo no es una escalera automática hacia la competitividad y la convergencia, como parecen argumentar Lefort y otros proponentes de esa fórmula de estatus, sino que incluso puede ser un impedimento al desarrollo de áreas críticas de la competitividad como la integración a la economía global y el desarrollo de un mercado de trabajo eficiente."

12. UNCTAD (2014) offers examples of local content requirements used in the energy sector across countries.

Chapter 3

Foreign Direct Investment under Fiscal Interdependence

When Policy Is Set Unilaterally[1]

There are country-specific cases which suggest that one of the benefits of attracting foreign multinational corporations is the jobs they create in the host country (e.g., Adams et al. 2014). Indeed, incentives to attract foreign corporations have been widely used to develop industry and create jobs (e.g., Lahiri and Ono 2004; Tolentino 2000). On the opposite side of the spectrum, there is evidence which suggests that job creation and the technology brought into the host country by foreign firms may be at the expense of welfare losses in the host country through, for example, environmental degradation (e.g., OECD 1999), the repatriation of profits and favoritism to firms from specific countries to establish operations in the host country (e.g., Svedberg 1981). This chapter looks not only at, *inter alia*, the gains from foreign direct investment, on the one hand, but also the potential losses arising from favoritism to firms from a specific country to establish operations in the host country.

Historically, the role of multinational corporations can not only be illustrated through the case of the food industry in countries like Colombia and Mexico, but also in the case of the pharmaceutical industry in economies such as Ireland, India and Puerto Rico, and the car industry in the United Kingdom. Specifically, the Puerto Rican economy experienced unprecedented growth through tax incentives US firms enjoyed as foreign corporations operating in Puerto Rico (Baumol and Wolff 1996; Dietz 2003; Ramcharran 2011). Recently, however, the Puerto Rican economy has suffered large job losses arguably because a relatively large number of firms left to establish operations elsewhere (Federal Reserve Bank of New York 2012; Ramcharran 2011, 396). Figure C.3 shows the downward trend in total employment in the manufacturing sector; real GDP in the economy also shows a decline along with labor productivity (Collins and Bosworth 2006, 35; Federal Reserve Bank of New York 2012).

This decline in employment can be partly attributed to the reduction in the tax incentives offered by the US federal government (Federal Reserve Bank of New York 2012; GAO 2014). Indeed, there is evidence in the literature for the close linkage between tax incentives and job creation via foreign direct investment in OECD countries and the European Union (e.g., Adams et al. 2014), and evidence that multinational corporations do react to tax incentives (e.g., Bénassy-Quéré et al. 2005; Mutti 2003). In spite of the rapid job loss and the lack of strong tax incentives by the US government[2] little attention has been given by policymakers in Puerto Rico to the potential benefits of acquiring additional controls over economic policymaking tools.[3] The present work seeks to fill this void from a theoretical perspective.

With these in mind, this chapter looks at the potential gains arising from job creation in the host country in industries which are oligopolistic in nature and, also, dominated by foreign firms which have established operations in the host country. I show that moving away from an equilibrium which entails a closer fiscal relationship between the host and foreign country is welfare-enhancing for both economies. The driver for this result is simply that a closer fiscal relationship implies the elimination of tax incentives to attract (and retain) foreign firms.[4] It is also shown that as companies operating in the host country see greater profit opportunities abroad, they leave the host country and establish operations elsewhere, thereby having a detrimental impact on the host country. In this context it is shown that it is in the best interest of the host and foreign country to work together as two separate economies, that is, under fiscal independence. The case where the host economy offers a subsidy to offset the costs of a closer fiscal scenario and attract foreign firms is examined; I show that in this case the foreign country gains at the expense of the subsidy offered by the host country, and that this subsidy is unsustainable as profit opportunities abroad increase.

The framework of analysis consists of two countries, a host and foreign country, where foreign, export-oriented firms operate in the host country. In the benchmark case welfare in the host country consists of employment creation exclusively, whereas the foreign country achieves welfare gains from the tax revenue arising from the production of foreign firms, which operate in the host country. What this set-up intends to capture is the case where the host country's welfare depends primarily on foreign firms. Additionally, the fiscal relationship is captured via a tax imposed on the production of foreign firms. The idea here is that under a closer fiscal relationship between the two economies firms operating in the host country would have to pay a relatively higher tax. A smaller tax, in contrast, represents the case where fiscal ties diminish. Even though this setting may warrant the analysis of policymaking in a non-cooperative set-up, issues of non-cooperation of tax policy have been analyzed elsewhere (e.g., Keen and Konrad 2013) and thus the focus of the present analysis is on issues of unilateral policy and the derivation of new results. Issues of profit taxation have also been studied elsewhere (e.g., Lahiri and Ono 2003).

In the context of the existing literature, there is a strand which looks at foreign direct investment and employment under imperfectly competitive markets (e.g., Adams et al. 2014; Barros and Cabral 2000; Brander and Spencer 1987; Kayalica and Yilmaz 2004; Lahiri and Ono 2003; Raff 2004;); and a second related strand at competition of profit shifting (e.g., Denicolò and Matteuzzi 2000; Fuest 2005; Janeba 1996, 1998, 2000; Lahiri and Ono 2004; Myles 1996). These strands look at issues of international tax/subsidy competition, strategic trade policy and foreign ownership; their analysis examines, among others, the conditions under which competing countries may enhance domestic welfare either via subsidies or a laissez-faire policy approach via a race to the bottom of local taxes.[5]

The contribution of this chapter is at the intersection of these two strands. In particular, the analysis examines the case where employment in the host country depends entirely on foreign firms operating in that country and, in addition, the incentives to attract foreign firms into the host country depend entirely on the foreign country's government. Issues of endogenous international tax competition (for a survey see e.g., Keen and Konrad 2013) or fiscal federalism (e.g., Bucovetsky 1991; Wildasin 1988) and strategic trade policy (e.g., Brander and Spencer 1987; Ishikawa and Spencer 1999) are put aside. Rather, the key issue at hand is employment considerations in one country and net tax revenue considerations in the second country, when policy is under the control of the latter. The goal of this chapter is to specifically analyze the potentially opposing interests between the host and foreign country when there is a unique fiscal relationship between the two.

With these in mind, Janeba (1996) shows, in a two-country model with imperfect competition in the output market, that the foreign government has an incentive to provide full tax credit if profits are completely repatriated. Barros and Cabral (2000) look at competition between countries to attract foreign direct investment via a subsidy and show, among others, that competition via subsidies may result in efficiency gains.[6] In contrast, the present chapter assumes that only one country has control over policy and so I do not model subsidy/tax competition as it is often times done in the literature. I also assume away issues of profit shifting since these have been analyzed extensively elsewhere. The reason for this departure is twofold. First, there is a small, though important, number of cases of economies which have practically no say on the implementation of policy even when this is the key for the creation of local jobs.[7] Second, the goal here is to characterize the policy offered by the host country in the case where the foreign country sets *a priori* the conditions of the fiscal relation between the two countries.[8]

The present chapter is closely related to the model of FDI in Kayalica and Yilmaz (2004) where the host country sets policy (tariff and output tax), profits are repatriated and the government cares about employment, tax revenue and consumer surplus. Welfare analysis is restricted to the host country. The authors show that when policy is set simultaneously a zero-tariff and output subsidy is optimal; this is consistent with results here. However, I extend the welfare analysis to a two-country model and focus on the opposing interests across countries. Furthermore, Lahiri and Ono (2003) examine the properties of the local content and FDI on welfare in the presence of unemployment. They show that the host country's welfare, which depends entirely on employment from foreign firms, may benefit from stricter requirements on the one hand, but on the other foreign firms may exit the market since they are required to employ less efficient inputs. Even though their model focuses on local content, it points out to two opposing effects a host government needs to weigh when employment is the key.[9]

In the context of US states, issues of trade restrictions and subsidy competition for FDI among states have been explored in the literature, for example, Adams et al. (2014). In their analysis the authors show, *inter alia*, that a (costly) positive subsidy for FDI is possible when states compete with each other for FDI. A key driver for this result is the presence of trade policy: the presence of a tariff may induce states to compete with each other for jobs in a costly fashion by offering higher subsidies to attract foreign firms. Although the subsidy as a policy to attract FDI is part of the present chapter, it differs crucially from Adams et al. in that (i) trade policy is assumed away in order to focus on the fiscal relation between two countries, (ii) welfare analysis incorporates the foreign country (i.e., the country of origin of FDI) and not just the host country as they do, and (iii) the goal of the present chapter is not to analyze exports versus location decisions by firms. What I want to analyze rather is the potentially opposing interests between the host and foreign country in the presence of a unique fiscal relationship where employment considerations are key to the host country.

The fourth strand this chapter contributes to is the rich literature on Puerto Rico's economy, where little attention has been given to the development of theoretical models to study its economy. Bosworth and Collins (2006), Baumol and Wolff (1996) as well as Dietz (2003) study the determinants of economic growth, and Sotomayor (2004) the effects of federal transfer policy on income inequality. Dunn (2011) studies empirically the relation between political dependence and development in a group of islands including Puerto Rico. Catalá (2013) and Dietz (1986) provide a historical perspective on the economy of Puerto Rico, including its institutional development. The issue of industrial policy and trade is touched by Lawrence and Lara (2006), where they argue that trade liberalization is not likely to hurt industries in Puerto Rico which do not operate under preferential trade treatment. This suggests that by opening the economy to a more liberal trade model, current industries are not likely to be negatively impacted. Dietz (2003) and GAO (1998, 2014) discuss the implications of federal tax incentives on the local economic and federal tax revenue (income and corporate taxes). None of these works delve into the analysis of the manufacturing sector and federal incentives from a theoretical perspective.

The rest of the chapter is structured as follows. The next section presents the model followed by the cases where firms are taxed and the host country offers a subsidy to attract foreign firms. The last section concludes.

THE MODEL

Consider n identical export-oriented foreign firms operating in the host country, which compete à la Cournot. Inverse market demand arises from preferences such that

$$p = \alpha - \beta \sum_i x_i \tag{3.1}$$

where x_i denotes output by foreign firm i ($i = 1, 2, ..., n$). Each firm i exhibits constant marginal costs, c_i, and is subject to a per-unit tax, t, for each unit of output, which is set unilaterally by the foreign country. Each firm maximizes profit by simultaneously choosing its level of output taking all other firms' output as given. In particular, each firm i solves

$$max\, \pi_i = (p - c_i - t\theta)x_i \tag{3.2}$$

Even though this type of per-unit tax is not new in the literature, it intends to capture the tax foreign firms operating in the host country pay to the foreign government. As pointed out in Brander and Spencer (1987, 265), an output tax affects "the employment issue most directly," a key aspect in this chapter. The positive constant θ captures exogenous non-economic factors (e.g., political or regulatory factors) and so the effective tax is given by θt; the role of θ is discussed in the last section. For example, even in the case where the tax makes sense from an economic standpoint, politicians may want to abolish the tax, that is, $\theta \approx 0$ for political reasons.

I shall follow Lahiri and Ono (2004) in that foreign firms will operate in the host country as long as they make at least a level of profits, $\tilde{\pi}_i$, that is, reservation level of profits. Since the host country is assumed to be small $\tilde{\pi}_i$ is assumed to be constant. If profits opportunities abroad for firm i, $\tilde{\pi}_i$, increase then firm i will exit the host country and establish operations elsewhere. This is consistent with evidence which suggests that large US corporations show a trend of moving operations overseas (Baily and Bosworth 2014). The free entry and exit of firms is thus captured by the following condition

$$\tilde{\pi}_i = \pi_i \tag{3.3}$$

Maximization of Equation (3.2) yields under symmetry the following first-order condition

$$p - c - \theta t = \beta x \tag{3.4}$$

This equation, along with Equation (3.3), determine the equilibrium level of output, x, and number of firms, n. I shall assume an interior solution throughout. In particular,

$$x = \sqrt{\tilde{\pi}_i/\beta} \tag{3.5}$$

$$n + 1 = \frac{\alpha - c - \theta t}{\beta\sqrt{\tilde{\pi}_i/\beta}} \tag{3.6}$$

Clearly, the effect of the tax works exclusively via the number of firms, meaning that a higher tax induces firms to exit the market due to higher tax payments and thus lower profits. As potential profits abroad, $\tilde{\pi}_i$, rise firms exit the market and so each foreign firm in the host country produces more, that is, $\partial n/\partial\tilde{\pi}_i < 0$ and $\partial x/\partial\tilde{\pi}_i > 0$.[10]

WELFARE

Consider two countries, namely, a home (host) and foreign country. Foreign firms operate in the host country, face no competition from host firms, and export the production of a homogeneous goods to a third market. Welfare in the host country depends on the income derived by the output generated by foreign firms. These are simplifying assumptions which intend to capture the important role of US firms in terms of employment creation abroad. I shall follow Lahiri and Ono (1998) and assume that the cost of production translates as income in the host country:

$$W^h = cnx \tag{3.7}$$

Welfare in the foreign country depends entirely on the revenue which arises from the tax foreign firms pay to the government of the foreign country. This set-up intends to capture the benefits to the US government arising from the tax revenue generated by US (foreign) firms operating abroad. That is,

$$W^f = \theta tnx \qquad (3.8)$$

A smaller tax, *ceteris paribus*, can be thought of as a case where the two countries relate to a lesser extent from a fiscal standpoint; that is, a small tax indicates that the fiscal interaction between economies in the type of industry modeled here is less. A relatively large tax denotes the case where the two economies relate relatively more from a fiscal standpoint.

The notion of a "fiscal relation" or "fiscal interaction" is specifically modeled based on the idea that tax revenue raised by the foreign country depends exclusively on the home country. For example, a positive tax denotes the tax revenue from US firms operating abroad (host country) to the US federal government. A relatively small (large) positive tax, *ceteris paribus*, denotes less (more) benefits in the form of revenue to the foreign country arising specifically from operations of foreign firms in the host country, and therefore a smaller (higher) degree of fiscal interaction.

The order of events is as follows. The foreign country chooses the tax so as to maximize W^f. Firms then take policy as given and maximize profits by choosing the level of output. Notice that by assumption the home country does not have a say on the choice of the tax. The choice of a tax to be paid to the US government is solely determined by the US government; this is a plausible assumption based on the discussion presented in the introductory section. In what follows it is important to keep in mind that the comparative statics analysis starts from an equilibrium which denotes a degree of fiscal interaction between the two countries. That is, the initial equilibrium is neither complete fiscal independence nor complete fiscal dependence. This initial set-up illustrates the extent to which the equilibrium moves to an equilibrium characterized by either more or less fiscal independence.

Non-cooperative Equilibrium

The characterization of the optimal tax, $t*$, which is set by the foreign country, is given by the maximization of Equation (3.8):

$$\frac{1}{\theta}\frac{\partial W^f}{\partial t} = nx + t\left(n\frac{\partial x}{\partial t} + x\frac{\partial n}{\partial t}\right) = 0 \Rightarrow t^* = \frac{\alpha - c - \beta x}{2\theta} > 0 \qquad (3.9)$$

where $\partial x/\partial t = 0$ and $\partial n/\partial t = -\theta/\beta x$, and W^f is a strictly concave function where at, $t = 0$, $\partial W^f/\partial t > 0$ thus indicating a positive optimal tax, $t*$.[11] To see the difference in incentives across countries arising from the tax, differentiation of Equations (3.7) and (3.8) gives

$$\frac{1}{c}\frac{\partial W^h}{\partial t} = t\left(n\frac{\partial x}{\partial t} + x\frac{\partial n}{\partial t}\right) \tag{3.10}$$

$$\frac{1}{\theta}\frac{\partial W^f}{\partial t} = nx + t\left(n\frac{\partial x}{\partial t} + x\frac{\partial n}{\partial t}\right) \tag{3.11}$$

where $\partial W^h/\partial t < 0$ and $W^h = cnx$ is a linear function of the tax. Figure C.4 summarizes some of the results from the analysis. First, it is noteworthy that the welfare maximizing tax for the host country is a zero-tax policy since this would result in more foreign firms operating in that country. Second, for the foreign country, however, there is an incentive to set a positive tax since it raises welfare in that country via tax revenue.[12]

Proposition 1: *Starting at the non-cooperative tax, t∗, welfare in the host country rises, but welfare in the foreign country falls with a decrease in the tax.*

Next, I examine differences in incentives across countries in setting the optimal tax arising from changes in profit opportunities abroad. The key result here is that as profit opportunities elsewhere improve, the number of foreign firms operating in the host country falls and, as a result, tax revenue in the foreign country diminishes; the foreign country thus responds by setting a lower tax in order to control the exit of firms from the home country. The analysis indicates that the incentives for the foreign country to set a tax diminish as foreign firms move abroad seeking higher profit opportunities. In other words, as profits opportunities abroad become sufficiently large the benefits to the foreign country, arising from the revenue in the home country, become negligible. Figure C.5 summarizes these results.[13] Figure C.5 shows, among others, the level of profits such that the optimal tax is very small; after this threshold the incentive to set a tax by the foreign country is nil and therefore the benefits to the foreign country associated with the host country become negligible.

It is noteworthy that as a result of foreign firms exiting the home country, and the resulting decrease in the optimal tax by the foreign country, the end result is an equilibrium where there is relatively less fiscal interaction. This reduction in the tax, although not sufficiently strong to avert a reduction in welfare in the host and foreign country, does minimize welfare losses. In particular, the change in welfare in the host and foreign country with respect to the reservation level of profits is given by

$$\frac{1}{c}\frac{\partial W^h}{\partial \tilde{\pi}} = n\frac{\partial x}{\partial \tilde{\pi}} + x\frac{\partial n}{\partial \tilde{\pi}} + x\frac{\partial n}{\partial t}\frac{\partial t}{\partial \tilde{\pi}} = -\frac{\partial x}{\partial \tilde{\pi}} + x\frac{\partial n}{\partial t}\frac{\partial t}{\partial \tilde{\pi}} \tag{3.12}$$

where $n\partial x/\partial\tilde{\pi} + x\partial n/\partial\tilde{\pi} = -\partial x/\partial\tilde{\pi} < 0$, and the last term denotes the effect on home's welfare via the adjustment of the tax as a result of a change in $\tilde{\pi}$. The effect of $\tilde{\pi}$ on foreign's welfare is given by

$$\frac{1}{\theta}\frac{\partial W^f}{\partial\tilde{\pi}} = t\left(n\frac{\partial x}{\partial\tilde{\pi}} + x\frac{\partial n}{\partial\tilde{\pi}}\right) + \frac{\partial t}{\partial\tilde{\pi}}\left(nx + t\left(n\frac{\partial x}{\partial t} + x\frac{\partial n}{\partial t}\right)\right) = -t\frac{\partial x}{\partial\tilde{\pi}} + tx\frac{\partial n}{\partial t}\frac{\partial t}{\partial\tilde{\pi}} + nx\frac{\partial t}{\partial\tilde{\pi}}$$

$$(3.13)$$

where the first term captures the effect on foreign's welfare via reductions in the tax revenue. The last two terms capture the effect via the tax adjustment as a result of a change in $\tilde{\pi}$, where the government needs to balance the effects on tax revenue via the exit of firms, on one side, and reductions in the revenue for a given tax base on the other.

Starting at $t*$, the home country experiences a reduction in welfare via the exit of firms, $-\partial x/\partial\tilde{\pi}$ in Equation (3.12), but at the same time an increase in welfare as a result of the tax adjustment by the foreign country, $x(\partial n/\partial t)(\partial t/\partial\tilde{\pi})$. The former effect offsets the latter and thus home's welfare falls as firms exit the market seeking higher profits. As a result, the foreign country experiences a decrease in welfare. In particular, at $t*$ Equations (3.12) and (3.13) become

$$\left.\frac{\partial W^h}{\partial\tilde{\pi}}\right|_{t=t^*} = -\frac{1}{2}\frac{\partial x}{\partial\tilde{\pi}} < 0 \qquad\qquad (3.14)$$

$$\left.\frac{\partial W^f}{\partial\tilde{\pi}}\right|_{t=t^*} = -\theta t\frac{\partial x}{\partial\tilde{\pi}} < 0 \qquad\qquad (3.15)$$

where from Equation (3.9) $\partial t/\partial\tilde{\pi} < 0$, and the last two terms in Equation (3.13) cancel out.[14]

Proposition 2: *Starting at the non-cooperative tax,* t*, *the gains from the host country that flow into the foreign country vanish as foreign firms exit the home country seeking higher profits elsewhere.*

Proposition 3: *There exists a reservation level of profits such that the non-cooperative tax is zero, that is, fiscal independence.*

Cooperative Equilibrium

Next, I look at the tax in a cooperative context. The key result here is that there are potential welfare gains for sufficiently large reservation level of profits under fiscal independence. Results from the analysis are in line with the literature.[15] The tax is derived from the maximization of total welfare, $W = W^h + W^f = nx(c + t\theta)$, which yields the following first-order condition

$$\frac{\partial W}{\partial t} = (c + t\theta)x\frac{\partial n}{\partial t} + xn\theta = 0 \Rightarrow t_0 = \frac{\alpha - c - \beta x}{2\theta} - \frac{c}{2\theta} \tag{3.16}$$

where the $W(\cdot)$ function is strictly concave and the coordinated tax, t_0, is less than the tax set by the foreign country unilaterally, $t*$; moreover, $t_0 > 0$ *if and only if* $c < (\alpha - \beta x)/2$, that is, marginal costs are sufficiently small. The reason the coordinated tax is positive under this condition is that the need to attract foreign firms to the home country via lower taxation is less if foreign firms are sufficiently efficient.

To show the potential welfare gains under fiscal independence for a sufficiently large reservation level of profits I shall use $0 < t_0 < t*$ and derive the reservation level of profits associated with welfare gains. This is illustrated in figure C.5; specifically, for $\tilde{\pi} \in [\tilde{\pi}_1 = (\alpha - 2c)/\beta, \tilde{\pi}_2 = (\alpha - c)^2/\beta]$ the tax, when set unilaterally by the foreign country, exceeds the coordinated tax associated with fiscal independence, that is, for sufficiently large reservation level of profits fiscal independence, $t_0 = 0$, raises global welfare.

Proposition 4: *There are welfare gains under fiscal independence for a sufficiently large reservation level of profits.*

WHEN A SUBSIDY IS OFFERED BY
THE LOCAL GOVERNMENT

One of the policy responses against the flight of firms is for the local government to offer a subsidy. I extend the analysis presented in the previous section by including a lump-sum subsidy payment by the local government to foreign firms operating in that country.[16] The analysis indicates that if such a subsidy is offered, then more foreign firms operate in the host country, thereby raising revenue in the foreign country. In terms of the optimal subsidy, there is a clear distinction between the interest of the foreign and host country. Figure C.6 summarizes this result. It is important to note that the subsidy is paid by the host government and thus it raises questions about how best to afford it. It is noteworthy that the optimal subsidy is positively related to the reservation level of profits, thereby putting extra pressure on the local government to keep foreign firms operating in the host country. The policy implication here is that the subsidy might be a viable option up to a point, since the cost of the subsidy may be too high as profit opportunities abroad improve.[17]

In the presence of a subsidy the order of events is as follows. The foreign country chooses the tax optimally so as to maximize W^f, and the home country takes that tax as given and chooses the subsidy that maximizes W^h. Firms then take policy as given and maximize profits by choosing the level of output in a Cournot-Nash fashion. The analysis focuses on the case where the optimal subsidy is positive since the focus is on the case where the host country tries to slowdown the exit of foreign firms. The assumption about the order of events seeks to capture the host country's government choice of the subsidy based on the tax or degree of fiscal dependence determined unilaterally by the foreign country. The model is solved using backwards induction.

The key difference in the solution of the profit-maximization problem, when compared to the no-subsidy case, is the equilibrium level of output by each firm obtained in the maximization problem. In particular, the profit-maximization problem is given by $max_{xi} \pi_i = (p - c_i - t\theta)x_i + S$, where S denotes the lump-sum subsidy, and therefore the first-order condition is analogous to Equation (3.4). The free-entry condition given in Equation (3.3) along with the first-order condition of firms yield, under symmetry, the equilibrium output, $x = [(\tilde{\pi} - S)/\beta]^{1/2}$, and number of firms, which is analogous to Equation (3.6). It can be shown that the number of firms rises with the subsidy due to higher profits, and as a result each firm's output falls, that is, $x_S = -1/2\beta x < 0$, $n_S = (\alpha - c - t\theta)/2\beta^2 x^3 > 0$, where subscript denote partial derivatives.

Non-cooperative Equilibrium

Consider the welfare functions in the presence of a lump-sum subsidy:

$$\max_{S} W^h = cnx - nS \tag{3.17}$$

$$\max_{t} W^f = \theta tnx \tag{3.18}$$

where S denotes the lump-sum subsidy to foreign firms operating in the host country. The home country chooses the subsidy so as to maximize (3.17), taking the tax as given; the first-order condition is characterized by $\partial W^h/\partial S = 0$. It can be shown (I delve into this point below) that the optimal subsidy is positive as long as it lies within a certain range of $\tilde{\pi}$. In particular, taking the tax of the foreign country as given, the first-order condition of the home country is given by $\partial W^h/\partial S = c(xn_S + nx_S) - n - Sn_S = -cx_S - n + Sx_S(n+1)/x = 0$, where $S > 0$ if and only if $\tilde{\pi}_0 > (2\alpha - c - t\theta)^2/4\beta$. I shall restrict the analysis to this range of positive subsidy in order to address the policy issue that motivates this section. As long as the subsidy is positive, it can be shown that the function $W^h(\cdot)$ is strictly concave. In this second stage, the maximization problem yields a subsidy as a function of the tax.

The foreign country maximizes (3.18), using the subsidy obtained from the second stage. The first-order condition for the foreign country yields $\partial W^f/\partial t = \theta t \, (x\partial n/\partial t + n\partial x/\partial t) + \theta t S_t \, (x\partial n/\partial S + n\partial x/\partial S) + \theta nx = 0$, where subscripts denote partial derivatives; thus assuming strict concavity in the $W^f(\cdot)$ function the optimal tax is positive since at $t = 0$, $\partial W^f/\partial t > 0$. Substituting the optimal tax, $t**$, back into $\partial W^h/\partial S = 0$ yields the optimal subsidy, $S^h = S^h(t**)$.

Having characterized optimal policy, figure C.6 shows the incentives of the foreign country vis-à-vis the host country, *viz.*, foreign has an incentive to set a relatively high subsidy at the expense of home. That is, given the optimal tax, the subsidy level the foreign country would set exceeds that of the home country, thereby resulting in a welfare reduction in the home country. The analysis also indicates that welfare in the foreign country falls as the subsidy approaches zero. The intuition is that a larger subsidy in home raises revenue in foreign at no cost to the foreign country.[18] Analogously, using $\partial W^f/\partial t = 0$, S^f denotes the subsidy satisfying $\partial W^h/\partial S = 0$, which in figure C.6 is positive as long as $\tilde{\pi} > (2a - c)^2/4\beta$.

Using the above analysis, I investigate how an exogenous change in the reservation level of profits affects the optimal subsidy for the home country, assuming that the tax remains fixed. In particular, the pressure on the host government to raise the optimal subsidy, resulting from an increase in profit opportunities abroad, builds up without any tax adjustment from the foreign country; the range of $\tilde{\pi}$ for which this happens is illustrated in figure C.7, that is, S^h is positive between $\tilde{\pi}_0$ and $\tilde{\pi}_{00}$ as shown in the dashed area in the figure.[19] The figure also shows $\tilde{\pi}_{00}$ as the value on the 45 degree line where $\tilde{\pi} = S^h$; recall that the non-negativity of x requires $\tilde{\pi} > S^h$ and so the value of S is bounded by $\tilde{\pi}_{00}$. If the reservation level of profits becomes large (i.e., exceeds $\tilde{\pi}_{00}$) subsidy payments become unsustainable for the host country.

Using this range the analysis indicates that, for a given tax, the host country raises the optimal subsidy as profits elsewhere rise. In particular, starting at $\tilde{\pi} \in (\tilde{\pi}_0, \tilde{\pi}_{00})$ differentiation of $\partial W^h/\partial S = 0$, where $\partial W^h/\partial S$ is a function of $S^h(\tilde{\pi})$, and $\tilde{\pi}$, yields

$$-W^h_{S^h S^h} \frac{\partial S^h}{\partial \tilde{\pi}} = W^h_{S^h \tilde{\pi}} = \frac{2}{x} \left(\frac{\partial x}{\partial S^h}\right)^2 (c - \beta nx) - \frac{\partial n}{\partial \tilde{\pi}} > 0 \qquad (3.19)$$

where $W^h_{S^h S^h} < 0$ from the concavity of $W^h(\cdot)$, $\partial n/\partial \tilde{\pi} < 0$ and $c - \beta nx > 0$ since $S^h > 0$. This case (i.e., for a given tax) is particularly relevant in a situation where the foreign government does not react to exogenous changes in the reservation level of profits. The implication here is that as the reservation level of profits becomes large (i.e., exceeds $\tilde{\pi}_{00}$) subsidy payments become unsustainable for the host country.

The pressure of subsidy payments on the host government may also arise from changes in the effective tax via θ. The idea here is that the effective tax may rise for political or regulatory reasons, for example, the foreign country unilaterally raises the tax seeking a close fiscal relation or cost-increasing regulations in the foreign country are applied to the home country. Intuitively, an increase in the effective tax (increase in θ) reduces the number of foreign firms operating in the host country. As a result, the host government responds with subsidy payments to avoid the exit of firms. In the standard case where the tax and subsidy are positive the change in the subsidy, S^h, is given by

$$-W^h_{S^h S^h} \frac{\partial S^h}{\partial \theta} = W^h_{S^h \theta} = \frac{t(S + 2\beta x^2)}{2\beta^2 x^3} > 0 \tag{3.20}$$

The relation between θ and S captures the interplay between political factors and subsidy payments in the home country.

Next, I look at the extent to which the host country changes its subsidy payments due to a change in the reservation level of profits via the tax. If the effective tax falls via t because, say, $\tilde{\pi}$ rises, then the subsidy falls as a result. This suggests that as profit opportunities abroad become large, the incentives to set a higher tax by the foreign country diminish thereby reducing the pressure by the host country to set a positive subsidy to attract firms. In particular, differentiation of $S^h = S^h(t(\tilde{\pi}), \tilde{\pi})$ gives (subscripts denote partial derivatives)

$$d S^h / d \tilde{\pi} = S^h_t t_{\tilde{\pi}} + S^h_{\tilde{\pi}} \tag{3.21}$$

where the sign of (3.21) is in general ambiguous. The term $S^h_{\tilde{\pi}} > 0$ is given by (3.19); and the term $t_{\tilde{\pi}} < 0$ is obtained differentiating $W^f_t(t(\tilde{\pi}), \tilde{\pi}) = 0 \Rightarrow - W^f_{tt}$ $t_{\tilde{\pi}} = -\theta x_{\tilde{\pi}} < 0$, since $x_{\tilde{\pi}} > 0$. The term S^h_t is obtained by differentiating $W^{h}_{S}{}^{h}$ $(S^h(t), t) = 0 \Rightarrow W^h_{S^h S^h} S^h_t = -n_t + S^h x^h_S n_t > 0$, since a positive optimal subsidy is assumed.

The first term in Equation (3.21) captures the interplay between the tax adjustment as $\tilde{\pi}$ rises and the subsequent adjustment in the subsidy; this term is negative because a decrease in the tax, resulting from a higher reservation level of profits, requires lower subsidy payments by the home government, which suggests that subsidy payments subside in an equilibrium characterized by relatively more fiscal independence. If this effect is large (small) then the home country lowers (raises) subsidy payments.

Proposition 5: *If the reservation level of profits is sufficiently large, then subsidy payments become unsustainable for the host country. Subsidy payments subside under fiscal independence.*

It is noteworthy that the opposing interests across the two countries about the optimal tax do not change in the presence of the subsidy, meaning that a zero-tax is in the best interest of the home country. This result is analogous to the one derived in the previous section.[20]

Cooperative Equilibrium

Next, I examine the tax-subsidy policy vis-à-vis the non-cooperative equilibrium. The key result here is that there are welfare gains from fiscal independence, particularly as the reservation level of profits becomes large.[21] To characterize the coordinated policy, global welfare, $W^h + W^f$, is maximized first with respect to the subsidy; this characterization is then used to maximize global welfare with respect to the tax. In particular,

$$\frac{\partial(W^h+W^f)}{\partial S} = (c + \theta t)\left(x\frac{\partial n}{\partial S} + n\frac{\partial x}{\partial S}\right) - n - S\frac{\partial n}{\partial S} = 0 \Rightarrow \tilde{S} = \tilde{S}(t) \quad (3.22)$$

The coordinated tax is chosen so as to maximize global welfare imposing the condition in Equation (3.22):

$$\frac{\partial(W^h+W^f)}{\partial t}\bigg|_{\tilde{S}} = (c + \theta t)x\frac{\partial n}{\partial t} + nx\theta - S\frac{\partial n}{\partial t} + \left((c + \theta t)\left(x\frac{\partial n}{\partial S} + n\frac{\partial x}{\partial S}\right) - n - S\frac{\partial n}{\partial S}\right)S_t$$

$$= \left((c + \theta t)x - S\right)\frac{\partial n}{\partial t} + nx\theta = 0 \quad (3.23)$$

whence, using Equation (3.22):

$$2\theta t = \alpha - 2c - 2\beta x \quad (3.24)$$

Using (3.24) in (3.22) yields the coordinated subsidy $S^{fb} = \tilde{\pi}/2$; hence, substituting S^{fb} into (3.24) gives the coordinated tax $2\theta t^{fb} = (\alpha - c - \beta(\tilde{\pi}/2\beta)^{1/2}) - c - \beta(\tilde{\pi}/2\beta)^{1/2}$, where $x = (\tilde{\pi}/2\beta)^{1/2}$. As in the case with no subsidy, the coordinated tax is positive if firms are sufficiently efficient, that is, $t^{fb} > 0 \Leftrightarrow c < (\alpha - \beta x)/2$.

Next, I compare policies with the non-cooperative equilibrium. First, Equation (3.22) at the non-cooperative subsidy, S^h, indicates that the coordinated subsidy exceeds the subsidy from the non-cooperative equilibrium (i.e., $S^{fb} > S^h$ as long as the tax is positive; that is,

$$\frac{\partial(W^h + W^f)}{\partial S}\bigg|_{S^h} = t\theta\left(x\frac{\partial n}{\partial S} + n\frac{\partial x}{\partial S}\right) > 0 \quad (3.25)$$

where S^h satisfies $\partial W^h/\partial S^h = 0$ from the non-cooperative equilibrium. Second, evaluating $\partial(W^h + W^f)/\partial t$ at the non-cooperative tax, t^{**}, indicates that the coordinated tax is smaller, that is, $t^{fb} < t^{**}$.

These results indicate that there are welfare gains in an equilibrium closer to fiscal independence. Using the closed-form solutions for the tax and subsidy it is easy to see that taxation falls and the subsidy rises as profit opportunities for foreign firms elsewhere improve; this is consistent with the result in the case where there is no subsidy, particularly as the reservation level of profits becomes large. Results also indicate that it is in the interest of the two countries to encourage foreign firms to invest in the home (host) country both via lower taxation (set by the foreign country) and subsidies (set by the home country) for any positive level $\tilde{\pi}$; this is because incentives raise employment in the home country and tax revenue in the foreign country. It is noteworthy that because of the opposing interests across countries subsidization for all values of $\tilde{\pi}$ contrasts with the non-cooperative subsidy where the subsidy is positive for a specific range of $\tilde{\pi}$; this suggests the need for subsidies to raise global welfare.

Proposition 6: *There are welfare gains under fiscal independence, particularly for sufficiently large reservation level of profits. There are also welfare gains under subsidy payments for any reservation level of profits.*

CONCLUSION

This chapter develops a partial equilibrium model to analyze the effects of export-oriented foreign firms operating in the host country. At the center of the analysis is that the host country's main (only) source of employment arises from foreign firms; the key component in the foreign country's welfare is the revenue it derives from foreign firms in the host country. A key difference with the literature is that part of the incentive scheme to promote employment in the host country is set unilaterally by the foreign government. In this setting it is shown that a zero-tax equilibrium is in the interest of the host country. This result follows through in the case where the foreign country is also the consuming country and subsidy payments are made available to the host country as a policy tool. In the present chapter a small-tax equilibrium represents the case where the foreign and host country relate to a lesser extent in the sense that the tax revenue that flows from the host country to the foreign country vanishes. This is what I refer to as an equilibrium of fiscal independence. The analysis is particularly relevant to the case of US possessions where the level of employment provided by foreign (American) corporations in oligopolistic industries has been at the center of policymaking. In some cases the level of employment in these sectors shows a sharp decline along with the demise of the relatively aggressive incentives for US corporations (Federal Reserve Bank of New York 2012); the analysis suggests that a more independent policymaking setting would benefit all parties.

Inevitably, the analysis rests on a set of assumptions which limits the generality of some results and which could be relaxed to expand the analysis. First, although some of the results follow through under a non-linear demand setting where demand is not too convex, relaxing the linearity assumption is a natural extension of the analysis. Therefore, results should be understood in that context. Second, the analysis does not take into account general equilibrium effects and other aspects such as the large transfer payments from the US government to low-income households in its possessions and its effects on employment in other sectors of the economy. The implications of labor mobility are not considered either; this is a potentially relevant extension of the model given the degree of labor mobility from US possessions to the US mainland. The analysis, however, focuses on an industry which is quite isolated in terms of forward and backward linkages (for the case of Puerto Rico see Dietz (2003)), but that it has had an important role in the development process of the economy, for example, financial and construction sectors. An extension along the lines of Ishikawa and Spencer (1999) is likely to add a new, richer dimension to the analysis. Third, the analysis does not model potential sources of unemployment such as labor productivity. In the case of Puerto Rico, for example, evidence suggests that in the manufacturing sector labor productivity has shown a reduction since 1975 (Collins and Bosworth 2006, 35). Labor productivity is important in that it may further exacerbate the employment effects arising from foreign corporations. Fourth, policy questions about the feasibility of a more diversified industry and product differentiation are not addressed here, even though they have been mentioned in the literature as important aspects for the manufacturing sector to recover (Ramcharran 2011). Another potential extension of the model is to endogenize the political process by modeling the choice of θ. This would help study potential offsetting effects between the economic and political objectives between the host and foreign country.

NOTES

1. This chapter is a re-print of (2017) "Foreign direct investment under fiscal interdependence when policy is set unilaterally" *International Economics and Economic Policy* 14(4): 579–599. doi: 10.1007/s10368-016-0358-y

2. Tax incentive schemes have been characterized by a set US federal tax credits for US firms operating in Puerto Rico. These incentives promoted the development

of the non-agricultural sector, for example, pharmaceutical, chemicals, drugs and electronics (Dietz 2003, 140–160). The development of industry and job creation depends on US unilateral policy. Thus, if these policies are phased out (e.g., Section 936 of the US Internal Revenue Services, the American Samoa Economic Development Credit), it is reasonable to expect US corporations to seek higher profits elsewhere.

3. To be fair, more autonomy to implement policies to improve Puerto Rico's economy has been present in the public debate and discussed in the literature, for example, Catalá (2010). The Federal Reserve Bank of New York's Report on Competitiveness of Puerto Rico's economy also touches on this point.

4. In the US-Puerto Rico case this result is consistent with the findings in a recent report by the General Accountability Office (GAO 2014) and consistent with the empirical literature (e.g., Bénassy-Quéré et al. 2005).

5. There is a third strand closely related to the present chapter (e.g., Barros and Cabral 2000; Bjorvatn and Eckel 2006; Haufler and Wooton 1999, 2006), which looks at the conditions under which investment incentives (i.e., subsidies and/or lower taxation) are optimal when countries compete for FDI. The contribution to this strand is discussed in subsequent sections. There is also an extensive literature which examines issues of FDI and strategic trade/environmental policies under Cournot conditions, for example, Kayalica and Lahiri (2005), Elliot and Zhou (2013), Sanna-Randaccio and Sestini (2012), Gautier (2017) and Bayındır-Upmann (2003) just to name a few.

6. Ishikawa and Spencer (1999) also show the potential efficiency gains from subsidies in vertical oligopolies in a two-country model.

7. The analysis applies to the case of the Marshall Islands, American Samoa, Bermuda and other small Caribbean economies. Examples of policy include the American Samoa Economic Development Credit for the tuna and processing industry (see 2014 Press release Congressman Faleomavaega, http://faleomavaega.house.gov/media-center/press-releases/senate-finance-committee-passes-two-year- extension-of-american-samoa). The Caribbean Basin Initiative (CBI) also exemplifies US unilateral policy in the Caribbean and Central America. The CBI provides a platform for US investment to flourish in the region while allowing for unilateral policy changes by the US government (Dean 2002; ITA 2000; USTR 2013). Country examples include Costa Rica, Guyana, El Salvador, Honduras and Jamaica (Dypski 2002).

8. As examples of policies set *a priori*, some US corporations are tax exempt because of tax rules set unilaterally by the US government (see Permanent Subcommittee on Investigations, "Offshore Profit Shifting and the U.S. Tax Code," http://www.hsgac.senate.gov/subcommittees/investigations/hearings/offshore-profit-shifting-and-the-us-tax-code).

9. Other papers in the literature under oligopoly examine the effects of local content requirements on cross-hauling, for example, Lahiri and Ono (2004), chapter 10. In a different strand of the theoretical literature Grossman and Iyigun (1995) show, in a general equilibrium setting, that if the return on the investment in the colonial sector is small, then the colonial power abandons the colony. In this sense I found consistent results in the present chapter, but in an oligopoly setting since the focus here is on a very specific type of imperfectly competitive market.

10. Comparative static results hold with general demand and cost functions. To see this profits are given by Equation (3.2), but now costs are a function $c(x)$ satisfying $c' > 0$, $c'' > 0$, and inverse market demand curve, $p = p(nx)$, satisfying $p' < 0$, $p'' > 0$ and $xn = X$. Profit maximization under symmetry gives $p + xp' - c' - \theta t = 0$, and the free entry and exit of firms is determined by $\tilde{\pi} = px - c(x) - xt\theta$. These implicitly determined the equilibrium $x = x(t, \tilde{\pi})$, $n = n(t, \tilde{\pi})$ and $X = nx$. Profits are assumed to be concave, $p'(n+1) + nxp'' - c'' < 0$, marginal revenue is decreasing in output, $2p' + nxp'' < 0$, and marginal profits fall with total output, $p' + xp'' < 0$. Total differentiation yields

$$\delta dx = - x^2 p'' \theta dt - x[p' + xp''] d\tilde{\pi}$$

$$\delta dn = -x[2p' + nxp'' - c''] \theta dt + [p'(n+1) + nxp'' - c''] d\tilde{\pi}$$

where $\delta > 0$ is the determinant of the coefficient matrix. Here output by each firm falls with the tax, whereas in the linear case (i.e., $p'' = 0$) such an effect is nil. In particular, $X_t < 0$, $x_t < 0$, $n_t < 0$, $x_{\tilde{\pi}} > 0$, $n_{\tilde{\pi}} < 0$, $X_{\tilde{\pi}} < 0$.

11. It can be shown that in the presence of consumer surplus and linear demand the foreign country's welfare, $W^t = CS(nx) + \theta nxt$, yields $\partial W^t / \partial t = 0 \Rightarrow t* = 0$, where CS denotes consumer surplus. Even though this result depends on the linearity assumption, it does indicate the possibility of a zero-tax regime. In a more general setting and analogous to Brander and Spencer (1987, 267), the optimal tax is small *if and only if* $-1 + P_X X_t = 0$ (subscripts denote partial derivatives) where demand is given by $P = P(X)$ and $X = nx$. That is, the optimal tax is small as long as the price increase due to the tax is close to unity. Even in this more general setting, the analysis points to the incentive the foreign country has to set a lower tax in the presence of consumer surplus, that is, a tax more in line with the home country's welfare maximizing conditions.

12. This result is in line with the literature on FDI which argues that countries will compete to attract foreign firms (FDI) via lower taxation. In figure C.4 $t^\wedge$ is simply the value of the tax so that $W^h = 0$. It can be shown that $t* < t^\wedge$.

13. Setting (3.11) equal to zero yields $t* = (\alpha - c - \beta x)/(2\theta)$. Hence, $\partial t*/\partial \tilde{\pi} < 0$; $t* \to (\alpha - c)/2\theta$ as $\tilde{\pi} \to 0$; $t* = 0 \Rightarrow \tilde{\pi} = (\alpha - c)^2/\beta$. Even though the foreign country could set a subsidy to keep firms exiting the host country, this case is ruled out; this is because as foreign firms move elsewhere the foreign country still gets tax revenue from the new location firms are operating at, where higher profits are generated.

14. In the general case Equation (3.14) holds and Equation (3.15) holds under mild conditions; a necessary and sufficient condition is derived to ensure $\partial t / \partial \tilde{\pi} < 0$. Consider welfare in the foreign country in Equation (3.8). Differentiation with respect to t gives (subscripts denote partial derivatives) $W_t^f = \theta(X + tX_t)$. Strict concavity of $W^f(\cdot)$ yields positive optimal tax. This is analogous to the linear case. The welfare function of the home country in Equation (3.7) yields $W_t^h = cX_t + Xc'x_t < 0$, that is, corner solution. The second term is not present in the linear; it simply compensates the first term via higher income. Then, total differentiation of $W_t^f(t(\tilde{\pi}), \tilde{\pi}) = 0$ yields

$$t_{\tilde{\pi}} = - W_{t\tilde{\pi}}^f / W_{tt}^f \quad \text{where } W_{t\tilde{\pi}}^f = \theta \left(X_{\tilde{\pi}} - \frac{X}{X_t} X_{t\tilde{\pi}} \right)$$

There are two effects: (i) an increase in $\tilde{\pi}$ induces a reduction in the tax to control for the exit of firms (the first term is negative), and (ii) the sign of the second term in $W^f_{t\tilde{\pi}}$ is ambiguous and new: it denotes the change in the tax base via the nonlinearities in the number of and output per firm. If the second term is small (i.e., demand is not too convex), then $t_{\tilde{\pi}} < 0$, that is, $|X_{\tilde{\pi}}| > | X_{t\tilde{\pi}} X / X_t |$. Next, differentiation of Equations (3.7) and (3.8) yields

$$\left.\frac{dW^f}{d\tilde{\pi}}\right|_{t=t^*} = \theta t X_{\tilde{\pi}} + \theta t_{\tilde{\pi}}(X + tX_t) < 0; \quad \left.\frac{dW^h}{d\tilde{\pi}}\right|_{t=t^*} = c(t_{\tilde{\pi}}X_t + X_{\tilde{\pi}}) + Xc'(t_{\tilde{\pi}}x_t + x_{\tilde{\pi}})$$

An exogenous increase in the reservation level of profits lowers welfare in the foreign country. In the home country, welfare falls if changes in income arising from more output are small (i.e., c' is small) and $t_{\tilde{\pi}}$ is small.

15. For example, Bjorvatn and Eckel (2006) and Barros and Cabral (2000) show that under intense competition (i.e., large reservation level of profits) incentives to attract firms raise welfare in the coordinated equilibrium. The key contribution here is that I derive the reservation level of profit under no taxation, that is, fiscal independence.

16. A lump-sum subsidy is used because it is a policy which influences entry/exit decisions while keeping the notion of fiscal interdependence, as defined in the present chapter, intact and thus facilitates comparison with results in previous sections.

17. Bjorvatn and Eckel (2006) show that the non-cooperative equilibrium may be characterized by investment incentives (i.e., subsidy) in the case where there is intense competition. In contrast, in the present model the subsidy is offered up to a threshold and actually becomes unsustainable if competition is too intense. Barros and Cabral (2000) show that in some cases welfare in one country rises, but falls in the other country, via subsidies; in the present model, however, both countries gain because welfare gains in one country translate to the other country.

18. The value of $S^f < 0$ in figure C.6 is obtained by using the optimal tax and differentiating W^f with respect to the subsidy. $W^f_t = 0$ gives t^{**}. Then, at t^{**} $W^f_S = \theta t/2\beta x > 0$, where $nx_S + xn_S = 1/2\beta x$; hence, $W^f_{SS} > 0$. For the host country the optimal subsidy will be positive as long as the subsidy payments do not exceed the gains in revenue. Formally, the optimal subsidy for the host country is positive *if and only if* $c - 2\beta nx > 0$.

19. Formally, $S^h > 0$ *if and only if* $\tilde{\pi}_0 > (2\alpha - c)^2/4\beta$. This condition is derived evaluating $\partial W^h/\partial S$ at $S = 0$ and solving for $\tilde{\pi}$ in $c - 2\beta xn > 0$, while keeping constant the optimal tax chosen by the foreign country.

20. At the optimal subsidy (i.e., using $W^h_S = 0$, the fact that $W^h = n(cx - S) > 0$ and $n_t < 0$), $W^h_t = (cx - S) nt < 0$ and $W^h_u = -n_tS_t > 0$, where differentiation of the first-order condition $W^h_S (S(t) , t) = 0$ yields $-W^h_{SS} St = W^h_{St} > 0$, where $W^h_{St} = (n_t X_S (-1+cx_S)) / (xn_S) > 0$ and $W^h_{SS} < 0$ from the concavity of the $W^h(\cdot)$ function.

21. Barros and Cabral (2000), Bjorvatn and Eckel (2006) and Haufler and Wooton (2006) show that under certain conditions about market size and degree of competition incentives (subsidies/lower taxation) raise welfare in the coordinated equilibrium. The contribution here is that, in the presence of fiscal interdependence, incentives via lower taxation and subsidies raise global welfare at any level of competition (i.e., reservation level of profits) to attract FDI.

Chapter 4

Unilateral Policy and Foreign Competition

This chapter examines aspects of increasing competition among firms which cater to the US market, and unilateral policies set by the United States which affect the extent to which firms have access to the US market. Because of the importance of the US market for Latin America and the Caribbean (LAC), plus the ongoing development of a number of bilateral agreements between the United States and LAC countries, the analysis of unilateral policies and access to the US market is relevant and timely.[1]

For example, free trade agreements between the United States and the Dominican Republic have lowered trade costs and therefore increased access to the US market of goods produced in the Dominican Republic (i.e., CAFTA-DR). Free trade is expected to take place between the United States and the Dominican Republic in an important number of industries. At the same time the US government has coupled market access with incentives to US companies operating in the Dominican Republic which export back to the United States (e.g., Caribbean Basin Initiative). The Dominican Republic has experienced rapid economic growth, and an increase in FDI particularly from the United States and Spain in advanced industries and services (UNCTAD 2009).[2]

In contrast, Puerto Rico already has complete access to the US market as well as access to incentives offered by the US federal government, but American companies which cater to the US market have been leaving Puerto Rico and relocating elsewhere. This seems to suggest that US FDI flowing into Puerto Rico has diminished.

These contrasting results may be partly due to the fact that companies exporting from the Dominican Republic to the United States do not face a number of regulations and taxes (which companies located in Puerto Rico face because Puerto Rico is part of US customs), thereby making companies in the Dominican Republic relatively more cost competitive. But also, the phasing out of special US federal incentive programs for American firms to establish operations in Puerto Rico has played an important role (e.g., IRS section 936). Changing regional and global market conditions (e.g., bilateral trade agreements have increased access to the US market and US FDI abroad) have arguably increased competition to attract US multinational companies.[3]

With these in mind, this chapter examines the policy reform of taxes and subsidies and the effects on output and profits of competing countries which cater to a third market. As an example, the United States sets policy unilaterally and firms which operate abroad and cater to the US market (e.g., Dominican Republic and Puerto Rico) react to and are affected by these policy reforms (with effects on industry performance).

The model consists of two sets of firms, one which operates in the home country and the other in the foreign country. Both sets of firms compete in a Cournot fashion for the production of an imperfect substitute which is exported entirely to a third market. Firms face (potentially different) per-unit taxes and subsidies, which are set by the third market's government. The analysis suggests that there are a number of policy reforms which can raise/lower output of foreign and home firms. But importantly, an equi-proportionate tax reduction is a policy reform which yields net benefits to all parties involved.

An equi-proportionate reduction in taxes faced by foreign and home firms unambiguously raises output for each of the two sets of firms and therefore industry output. This increase in industry output, in turn, yields a clear benefit to the export (receiving) country without any additional budgetary burden: a tax reduction does not represent an additional budgetary burden to the country setting taxes and subsidies to both sets of firms (e.g., the United States), and at the same time enjoys the benefits from additional industry output. Analogously, a policy reform consisting of additional subsidies raises foreign, home and therefore industry output, but at the same time raises budgetary pressures to the country setting policy.

I also explore other policy reforms and show that losses in market share, arising from preferential policies to one set of firms, can be minimized via a higher degree of product differentiation. This is because with more differentiated products differences in cost competitiveness across the two sets of firms become negligible. However, as firms produce more similar products (i.e., homogeneous goods) the cross-effects of policy become prominent. This result is important because as competing countries become important players in the US export market, Puerto Rico may experience increasingly a loss in market share as bilateral trade agreements take place and competing countries move up in the value-added production chain.

In the context of the US-Puerto Rico political and economic relationship, and consistent with chapter 3, higher taxation can be interpreted as a situation where Puerto Rico moves closer to a statehood-like equilibrium. For instance, if home firms are assumed to be US firms operating in Puerto Rico, then a higher tax can be interpreted as an equilibrium closer to statehood since under statehood firms operating in Puerto Rico will face higher taxes. This is important because results suggest that an equilibrium away from statehood (i.e., lower taxes) is beneficial across the board. This simply points to the need for moving toward an equilibrium consistent with political independence (i.e., national sovereignty) for Puerto Rico, that is, an equilibrium mutually beneficial for the United States and Puerto Rico.

The rest of the chapter is structured as follows. The next section presents the model set-up, followed by the comparative statics analysis. Results from the welfare analysis are then presented. The last section concludes with a brief discussion of policy implications and suggestions for future research.

THE MODEL

Consider a fixed number of m (n) firms operating in the foreign (home) country. Firms compete in a Cournot fashion for the production of an imperfect substitute which is exported entirely to a third market. Each set of firms can be thought of as US firms operating abroad which then export production back to the US market.

Demand faced by each firm i ($i = 1,2, \ldots , n$) operating in the home country and each firm j ($j = 1,2, \ldots , m$) operating in the foreign country is, respectively, given by

$$p^h = \alpha - \beta\left(q_1^h + q_2^h + \cdots + q_n^h\right) - \gamma\left(q_1^f + q_2^f + \cdots + q_m^f\right) \qquad (4.1)$$

$$p^f = \alpha - \beta\left(q_1^f + q_2^f + \cdots + q_m^f\right) - \gamma\left(q_1^h + q_2^h + \cdots + q_n^h\right) \qquad (4.2)$$

where q_l^k denotes output of firm l in country k, where $l = i, j$ and $k = h, f$. The constant γ denotes the degree of product differentiation where $0 < \gamma < \beta$, where in the case of homogeneous goods $\gamma = \beta$ and in the case of completely differentiated products $\gamma = 0$.

Each home firm i faces an output tax, t^h, and output subsidy, s^h, and costs are given by a cost function $c_i^h (q_i^h)$ which satisfies $c^{h\prime} > 0$, $c^{h\prime\prime} > 0$ $\forall$ i. Similarly, each foreign firm j faces a tax, t^f, and subsidy, s^f, and exhibits an analogous cost structure: $c^f(q_j^f)$ which satisfies $c^{f\prime} > 0$, $c^{f\prime\prime} > 0$ $\forall$ j. It is noteworthy that it is assumed that the government uses two policies to address one market distortion, that is, via a tax/subsidy combination, a policy scheme used frequently in industrial policy. The reason for this modeling strategy is twofold. First, it facilitates the analysis of policy reform; that is, to look specifically at tax/subsidy combinations across countries. And second, it captures the nature of policy combinations utilized by the United States to influence the behavior of US firms operating abroad.

Each firm $l = i,\ j$ operating in country $k = h,\ f$ maximizes profits in a Cournot-Nash fashion by choosing the level of output. In particular, each firm solves the following maximization problem:

$$\min_{q_l^k} \pi_l^k = p^k q_l^k - c_l^k\left(q_l^k\right) - q_l^k t^k + q_l^k s^k \tag{4.3}$$

The order of events is as follows. First, the government in the third market simultaneously chooses the policy vector, t^h, t^f, s^h, s^f. It is noteworthy that the governments of the countries in which firms operate do not have a say on the determination of policy. This assumption is to capture the unilateral nature of policy setting, which is a key element of analysis in the model. Second, each firm l operating in country k then takes policy as given so as to maximize profits by choosing the level of output. The model is solved by backwards induction. I shall assume an interior solution throughout and symmetry within each set of firms.

In particular, (4.3) yields two first-order conditions (one for each set of firms) which under symmetry are given by

$$p^h - \beta q^h - c^{h'} - t^h + s^h = 0 \tag{4.4}$$

$$p^f - \beta q^f - c^{f'} - t^f + s^f = 0 \tag{4.5}$$

where $p^h = \alpha - \beta n q^h - \gamma m q^f$, $p^f = \alpha - \beta m q^f - \gamma n q^h$. Consistent with the literature (e.g., Dixit 1986) stability and uniqueness of the Cournot equilibrium are ensured by assuming (subscripts denote partial derivatives) $\pi^h_{q^h q^h}$ $\pi^f_{q^f q^f}$ $-\pi^h_{q^h q^f} \pi^f_{q^f q^h} = (\beta(m+1) + c^f)\ (\beta(n+1) + c^h) - mn\gamma^2 > 0$, $\pi^h_{q^h q^h} = -(\beta(n+1) + c^h) < 0$, and $\pi^f_{q^f q^f} = -(\beta(m+1) + c^f) < 0$.

This completes the description of the model.

COMPARATIVE STATICS

Before going into the comparative statics analysis several remarks about the interpretation of the tax are in order. This will also be useful in the welfare analysis. In the context of the US-Puerto Rico political and economic relationship, higher taxation can be interpreted as a situation where Puerto Rico moves closer to a statehood-like equilibrium (this is analogous to the interpretation presented in chapter 3). For instance, if home firms are assumed to be US firms operating in Puerto Rico, then a higher tax, t^h, can be interpreted as an equilibrium closer to statehood since under statehood firms operating in Puerto Rico will face higher taxes. In contrast, lower taxation characterizes an equilibrium away from a statehood-like equilibrium. Now, foreign firms are assumed to be US firms operating abroad (e.g., Dominican Republic) and so a higher tax, t^f, simply means relatively less cost competitive firms; it does not mean that US firms operating in the foreign country are moving closer to a statehood-like equilibrium. The difference between taxation t^f and t^h simply captures the nuances of the Puerto Rico-US relationship.

As for subsidy payments, subsidies have an analogous interpretation across both sets of firms: higher subsidy payments aim at reducing production costs of foreign and home firms, but higher subsidies faced by home firms, s^h, may be interpreted as an equilibrium closer to statehood. It is noteworthy that both the tax and subsidy are set unilaterally by the third (importing) market (e.g., United States). The welfare properties of these policies are examined in the next section, where the interpretations of the tax and subsidy are important to capture the particulars of the US-Puerto Rico relationship.

With these in mind differentiation of (4.4) and (4.5) gives the following system

$$
\begin{bmatrix} -(\beta(n+1)+c^{h''}) & -m\gamma \\ -n\gamma & -(\beta(m+1)+c^{f''}) \end{bmatrix} \begin{bmatrix} dq^h \\ dq^f \end{bmatrix} = \begin{bmatrix} dt^h - ds^h \\ dt^f - ds^f \end{bmatrix} \tag{4.6}
$$

where the determinant of the coefficient matrix is given by $\eta = (\beta(m+1) + c^f$ $)$ $(\beta(n+1) + c^h) - mn\gamma^2 > 0$. The effects of the tax and subsidy on home and foreign output are therefore given by

$$
\eta dq^h = -(\beta(m+1) + c^{f''})(dt^h - ds^h) + m\gamma(dt^f - ds^f) \tag{4.7}
$$

$$
\eta dq^f = -(\beta(n+1) + c^{h''})(dt^f - ds^f) + n\gamma(dt^h - ds^h) \tag{4.8}
$$

An increase in the tax, t^h (subsidy, s^h) faced by home firms lowers (raises) output by home firms since a tax (subsidy) renders home firms relatively less (more) cost competitive. As a result, foreign firms react strategically by increasing (decreasing) output. An analogous analysis applies to a change in the tax/subsidy faced by foreign, t^f, s^f. Additionally, industry output, $nq^h +$ mq^f, falls (rises) with an increase in the tax (subsidy) faced by either firm, that is, an increase in either t^h or t^f; s^h or s^f. It is noteworthy that as products become very differentiated ($\gamma \simeq 0$) the cross effects of policy become negligible as differences in costs competitive disappear. These results are standard in the literature (e.g., Lahiri and Symeonidis 2007; Gautier 2013, 2014).

There are several policy reforms with interesting policy implications. First, an equal increase in the tax and subsidy faced by home firms (i.e., $dt^h = ds^h$) does not change home and foreign output. This is because with an equal policy change the effect on profits, and therefore output, cancel out; the strategic reaction of firms also cancels out. Industry output does not change in this case. Second, an equi-proportional increase in taxes (i.e., $dt^h = dt^f$) lowers home, foreign and therefore industry output. This is because the cross effects of the tax is completely offset, thereby lowering output of both sets of firms. An analogous analysis applies to the subsidy when it changes in an equi-proportional fashion.

Proposition 1: *An equi-proportional increase in the tax (subsidy) unambiguously lowers (raises) home, foreign and industry output.*

One policy implication here is that a reduction in taxes boosts output of foreign and home firms, and raises industry output. Thus all parties involved benefit from this policy reform. In contrast, even though an increase in the subsidy raises output, larger subsidies may create budgetary pressures to the country making subsidy payments. It is noteworthy that although there are a number of policy reforms which yield higher industry output, the impact on the individual set of firms may not necessarily be clear-cut. As a result, proposition 1 puts forward a policy reform which unambiguously raises output for each set of firms and the industry, while not putting budgetary pressure on the government for more subsidies. This policy reform is consistent with an equilibrium away from statehood for Puerto Rico.

Combining the effects of taxes and subsidies, consider an increase in the subsidy and tax faced by home firms, while leaving the tax and subsidy faced by foreign firms unchanged, that is, $dt^h > 0$, $ds^h > 0$, $dt^f = 0$, $ds^f = 0$. Then, home output increases *if and only if* the subsidy increase is large. Industry output rises under this condition while foreign output falls. The effect on foreign output is negligible as products become very differentiated (i.e., $\gamma \simeq 0$).

In the context of Puerto Rico a key policy implication is that, should Puerto Rico move closer to an equilibrium where it joins the United States as a state and, therefore, taxes increase, then output by firms operating in Puerto Rico rises only as long as the increase in subsidies is sufficiently large. It is noteworthy that although higher taxes may potentially fund subsidy payments, this scenario is unlikely as suggested in GAO (2014), that is, the US federal government will likely experience a relatively small increase in net subsidy payments to Puerto Rico should the island join the Union.

Importantly, this result also suggests (along with proposition 1) that output could be raised without the need for higher subsidy payments, but rather via a tax reduction. A tax decrease, in turn, is associated with a scenario which moves the Puerto Rican economy away from a statehood-like equilibrium. This result is stated in the following proposition.

Proposition 2: *A policy reform consisting of higher taxes and subsidies faced by home firms increases output of home firms if and only if subsidy payments are sufficiently large.*

To build from this line of reasoning, consider the policy reform $dt^f < 0$, $dt^h > ds^h > 0$, that is, foreign firms experience a reduction in taxes while home firms experience a sufficiently large increase in taxes. In this case industry output falls if the tax effect on home firms is sufficiently large. The implication here is that an increase in t^h results in a reduction in home output thereby putting pressure on the government to lower taxes faced by foreign firms and/or raise subsidy payments to home firms sufficiently. In the context of Puerto Rico, if a higher tax is characterized by a statehood-like equilibrium, then larger subsidy payments are likely to take place in order to aid local industry within the United States. Subsidy payments will yield budgetary pressures, however. If subsidy payments do not rise and tax incentives are offered to foreign firms, then the local industry (i.e., home firms) would still be affected negatively.

As a potential policy reform consider the case where aid to home firms is funded via higher taxation imposed on foreign and home firms, that is, $ds^f = 0$, $ds^h = dt^h + dt^f > 0$. In this case home output rises via an increase in the tax on foreign firms which finances subsidy payments to home firms, but foreign output falls as the foreign tax is raised to finance subsidy payments to home firms. Industry output thus falls if the reduction in foreign output is sufficiently large (i.e., *if and only if* $n(\beta(m+1) + c^{h\prime\prime}) > m(\beta(n+1) + c^{f\prime\prime})$). In the special case where production costs are linear (i.e., $c^{f\prime\prime} = 0$, $c^{h\prime\prime} = 0$), industry output falls *if and only if* the number of home firms is relatively large, that is, $n > m$. If the number of firms is identical ($n = m$) and costs are non-linear, then the condition reduces to $c^{f\prime\prime} < c^{h\prime\prime}$. In the context of Puerto Rico this condition on costs is particularly relevant since, relative to potential competitors, Puerto Rico is likely to exhibit higher marginal costs (particularly under statehood) at high production levels (i.e., relatively convex cost functions). As a result, funding subsidy payments may require higher taxation, which results in lower industry output.

In particular, under the policy reform $ds^f = 0$, $ds^h = dt^h + dt^f > 0$ the change in industry output is given by

$$\eta d(nq^h + mq^f) = [n(\beta(m+1) + c^{f\prime\prime}) - m(\beta(n+1) + c^{h\prime\prime})]dt^f \quad (4.9)$$

where the first (second) term denotes the change in industry output via changes in home (foreign) output.

Proposition 3: *Suppose subsidy payments going to home firms are funded via higher taxation on both home and foreign firms (i.e., $ds^f = 0$, $ds^h = dt^h + dt^f > 0$). Then, industry output falls if the reduction in foreign output is sufficiently* *large due to relative market conditions and cost structures, that is,* $n(\beta(m+1) + c^{h''}) > m(\beta(n + 1) + c^{f''})$.

WELFARE

This section characterizes optimal policy. As mentioned earlier, policy is set unilaterally by the third (importing) market via social welfare maximization. There are several important elements of analysis. First, in the current model the government faces one market distortion (i.e., output distortion) which it seeks to address via two policies (tax and subsidy). Normally, only one policy would be needed to address one distortion, but the presence of the tax and subsidy is due to the research objective of this chapter: the tax and subsidy help characterize, from an economic and political standpoint, the extent to which foreign and home firms are close to the third market. Therefore, it is the combination of a tax and subsidy which I am interested in, that is, $s^h - t^h$ and $s^f - t^f$.

The government of the third (importing) market solves the following welfare maximization problem:

$$\max_{t^h,s^h,t^f,s^f} W = CS(nq^h, mq^f) + n\pi^h + m\pi^f - mq^f s^f - nq^h s^h + mq^f t^f + nq^h t^h$$

$$(4.10)$$

where CS denotes consumer surplus. Differentiation of (4.10) gives

$$dW = -nq^h dp^h - mq^f dp^f + (p^h - c^{h'})ndq^h + (p^f - c^{f'})mdq^f + nq^h dp^h + mq^f dp^f$$

$$= (\beta q^h + t^h - s^h)ndq^h + (\beta q^f + t^f - s^f)mdq^f$$

$$(4.11)$$

where $p^h - c^h = (\beta q^h + t^h - s^h)$, $p^f - c^f = (\beta q^f + t^f - s^f)$.

Maximization of (4.10) with respect to t^h, t^f, s^h, s^f gives a system of four equations in four unknowns, which implicitly determine the optimal policy vector, and from which it can be shown that (see the Appendix A to this chapter for a detailed derivation):

$$\beta q^h = s^h - t^h \qquad\qquad\qquad (4.12)$$

$$\beta q^f = s^f - t^f \qquad\qquad\qquad (4.13)$$

In words, the government sets a tax/subsidy combination such that it addresses the output distortion associated to each set of firms. The extent to which the tax is smaller and subsidy larger depends upon the weight the government puts on these two policies to address the output distortion and, also, the weight it puts on promoting foreign output vis-à-vis home output.

For instance, if the output distortion associated to foreign firms is large (i.e., βq^f large), then the spread between the tax and subsidy is large, that is, via a combination of higher subsidy payments and/or lower taxation the output distortion is addressed (the difference $s^f - t^f$ becomes larger).

With these in mind it can be shown that the spread between the tax and subsidy is relatively large for the set of firms which exhibits smaller unit costs. The implication of this result is that the government of the importing market further incentivizes (via a combination of higher subsidies and/or lower taxation) the production of firms which are relatively more cost efficient. In the context of the US-Puerto Rico relationship this result suggests that if firms operating in Puerto Rico lose their competitiveness (e.g., are less cost competitive), then incentives coming from the United States are likely to diminish. Specifically, for a given tax, t^h, subsidy payments, s^h, are relatively smaller if home firms exhibit larger unit costs, c^h.

To see this result I shall assume constant marginal cost, $c^h = \tilde{c}^h$, $c^f = \tilde{c}^f$, where $\tilde{c}$ is a positive constant. This cost structure allows to obtain closed-form solutions for output q^h, q^f. In particular, with constant marginal cost, substituting (4.12) and (4.13) into the first-order conditions (4.4) and (4.5), home and foreign output are given by

$$nq^h = \frac{(\alpha - \tilde{c}^h)\beta - \gamma(\alpha - \tilde{c}^f)}{\beta^2 - \gamma^2} \tag{4.14}$$

$$mq^f = \frac{(\alpha - \tilde{c}^f)\beta - \gamma(\alpha - \tilde{c}^h)}{\beta^2 - \gamma^2} \tag{4.15}$$

whence $nq^h < mq^f \Leftrightarrow \tilde{c}^h > \tilde{c}^f$. That is, as foreign firms exhibit lower unit costs they enjoy a larger share of the market, thereby prompting the government to set policy to promote output via higher subsidies and/or lower taxation, that is, $s^f - t^f > 0$, $s^h - t^h > 0$. The government here is simply promoting production of the most efficient set of firms.

Proposition 4: *The government of the import market will promote relatively more efficient firms.*

CONCLUSION

This chapter presents a partial equilibrium model where foreign and home firms compete for the production of an imperfect substitute under Cournot conditions. The analysis suggests that a policy reform of stricter lower taxes for both sets of firms raises home, foreign and industry output. Even though a subsidy also yields increases in output, it is a less desirable policy prescription since it may put budgetary pressures on the government setting policy. In terms of welfare it is shown that incentives are more likely to be allocated to those firms which are relatively more cost efficient; in particular, for a given tax more efficient firms are likely to face higher subsidies.

In the context of the Puerto Rican economy results have several important policy implications. First, a smaller tax regime is associated with an outcome away from a statehood-like equilibrium. And a smaller tax regime makes all parties involved better off by raising output and addressing the output distortion without creating budgetary pressures. Therefore, an equilibrium consistent with political independence for Puerto Rico is in the best interest of all parties involved. Second, countries with lower cost structures (i.e., more cost competitive) are likely to obtain further incentives from the United States because in this way, output is produced in a more efficient way, thereby increasing the benefits to the United States (the import market) via higher production. The implication here is that, given the increase in foreign competition, Puerto Rico may experience less assistance from the United States in the form of subsidy payments. This poses a challenge to policymakers in Puerto Rico: it is difficult to make the case for Puerto Rico to get further assistance (subsidies) to cater the US market as long as cost structures in Puerto Rico are not sufficiently competitive. One way forward is to focus on cost competitiveness via investments in innovation, new infrastructure and the development of new technology. Again, the implication here is that political independence for Puerto Rico is consistent with a scenario where Puerto Rico is more cost competitive. Third, increasingly Puerto Rico's competitors are engaging in bilateral trade agreements with the United States and, therefore, gaining further access to the US market as well as special treatment in the form of subsidy/tax breaks are unlikely to remain a distinct competitive advantage feature for Puerto Rico. This, in turn, is deteriorating Puerto Rico's competitive position. The analysis suggests that these effects could be minimized by promoting the production in Puerto Rico of differentiated products as well as moving forward with an industrial development strategy consistent with political independence for Puerto Rico.

NOTES

1. See Bown and Crowley (2016) for a list of bilateral agreements where the United States participates.

2. Investment Policy Review: Dominican Republic, UNCTAD 2009, http://unctad.org/en/Docs/iteipc20079 en.pdf

3. More generally, the literature has underscored the increase in competition among developing countries to attract FDI, for example, Kayalica and Yilmaz (2004).

Chapter 5

Lobbying in the Presence of Foreign Competition

Industry lobbying and its effect on policy setting has been studied in the literature from a theoretical and empirical standpoint (e.g., Kang 2015; Grossman 2015; Bellemare and Carnes 2015; Bombardini and Trebbi 2012; Betrand, Bombardini and Trebbi 2011; Grossman and Helpman 2001; Dixit, Grossman and Helpman 1997). The literature suggests that lobbying efforts do influence, at least to an extent, policy setting. Moreover, in the context of Puerto Rico's economy the extent to which the United States sets policy is likely to depend, among others, upon the lobbying efforts by foreign, American firms operating in Puerto Rico. For example, Suarez (1998) describes the strategic behavior of a number of pharmaceutical and electronic US companies to protect tax breaks directly linked to their operations in Puerto Rico. This chapter thus presents a model to analyze lobbying by foreign firms and its effects on the country hosting the foreign firms.

The analysis indicates that foreign firms will lobby the foreign country (which sets policy unilaterally) to set policy consistent with higher profits for foreign firms. Moreover, increased pressure by the host country on foreign firms to employ resources from the host country results in additional incentives to the foreign country to lower taxation facing foreign firms. These results, therefore, suggest that an equilibrium characterized by lower taxation (i.e., a scenario away from a statehood-like equilibrium for Puerto Rico) is likely to arise as lobbying takes place. This is consistent with the results derived in chapter 3, but here the key factor driving the results is the lobbying efforts by the foreign industry.

There are no works in the literature which explore lobbying in the case of Puerto Rico from a theoretical perspective. Thus, the present analysis seeks to shed light on the political-economy issues in the Puerto Rico-US relationship and hopefully encourage future research in this area.

There are several policy implications from the analysis. First, policies presently set by the Puerto Rican government to create jobs are encapsulated in either tax cuts and/or subsidy schemes. This scenario raises questions about the ability of the government of Puerto Rico to offset economic shocks and promote economic activity, particularly since key economic policies are set unilaterally by the US Congress. Second, even as the US economy benefits from Puerto Rico's economic activity (e.g., via consumer surplus effects and tax revenue) the analysis indicates that an increase in taxation (faced by American firms operating in Puerto Rico) is unlikely to take place because of the lobbying efforts by the industry. From a political standpoint, and given the important role of American firms in the Puerto Rican economy, it is unlikely that a move toward statehood (i.e., higher taxation) will occur in the absence of additional aid from the US government (e.g., subsidies, tax credits). Additional aid, in turn, is extremely unlikely at the present time as signaled by recent legislation in the US Congress.[1]

The analysis presented in this chapter follows very closely Lahiri and Ono (2004, chapter 7). The key contribution to their work is that (i) a tax and are considered as policies, whereas in their analysis the local content is the only policy available to the government and (ii) policy consists of the foreign country setting the tax unilaterally. The interplay between the tax, local content and political contributions is explored in the present analysis. The model set-up consists of two sets of firms operating in the home (host) country, which compete à la Cournot for the production of a homogeneous good which is exported to the foreign (export) market. The government of the foreign country sets policy unilaterally in the presence of lobbying by foreign firms operating in the home country.

The rest of the chapter is structured as follows. The next section spells out the model, followed by the characterization of the political equilibrium. The comparative statics results are then presented. The last section presents concluding remarks along with a discussion of policy implications and potential extensions of the model.

THE MODEL

This section presents the model set-up in the absence of any political contributions, followed by the political contribution component of the model.

Consider a fixed number m (n) of foreign (home) firms operating in the home country. The number of foreign firms can be thought of as foreign direct investment. Firms (foreign and home firms) compete for the production of a homogeneous good, which is exported entirely to the foreign country's market, in a Cournot-Nash fashion.

Foreign (home) firms exhibit constant marginal cost c^f (c^h). Home firms employ inputs from the home market exclusively, but foreign firms may employ inputs from the home and foreign markets. k^h (k^f) denotes marginal cost of home (foreign) firms when production takes place using inputs from the home (foreign) country exclusively. The government in the home country may command foreign firms to employ a share δ of home inputs. Hence, marginal costs for the home and foreign firms are given, respectively, by

$$c^h = k^h \tag{5.1}$$

$$c^f = (1 - \delta)k^f + \delta k^h \tag{5.2}$$

where $\delta \in (0,1)$ and $k^h > k^f \Leftrightarrow c^h > c^f$. I shall assume $k^h > k^f$; this is to capture the idea that foreign firms are relatively more efficient than home firms and, also, to explicitly model the role of the local content requirement, δ, on the foreign firm's cost structure.[2] In addition to the local content, foreign and home firms face a per-unit (identical) tax, t. The role of the tax is analogous to that in chapter 3.

Demand faced by each home firm i (i = 1,2, ..., n) and foreign firm j (j = 1,2, ..., m) is given by

$$p = \alpha - \beta(q_1^h + \cdots + q_n^h) - \beta(q_1^f + \cdots + q_m^f) \tag{5.3}$$

where q^h_i denotes output by home firm i and q^f_j output by foreign firm j. I assume away issues of product differentiation which I touched on in chapters 4 and 6.

The government of the foreign country sets the tax (welfare maximization in the presence of political contributions is explained below). Firms (foreign and home) then take the tax as given and maximize profits. I shall assume an exogenous level of the local content and any issues of policy setting by the home country's government. This assumption is to focus the analysis on aspects of lobbying and policy setting by the foreign country. I shall assume interior solutions and symmetry within each set of firms.

Each home and foreign firm chooses output in a Cournot-Nash fashion so as to maximize profits. That is, each firm solves the following maximization problem:

$$\max_{q_l^k} \pi_l^k = \left(p - c_l^k - t\right)q_l^k \quad where \quad l = i, j; k = h, f \tag{5.4}$$

Differentiation yields, under symmetry, the following first-order condition for home and foreign firms, respectively:

$$p - c^h - t - \beta q^h = 0 \tag{5.5}$$

$$p - c^f - t - \beta q^f = 0 \tag{5.6}$$

where $p = \alpha - \beta(nq^h + mq^f)$. Equations (5.5) and (5.6) determine the equilibrium level of output q^h and q^f; in particular,

$$q^h = \frac{(\alpha - c^h - t) - m(1-\delta)(k^h - k^f)}{\beta(m+n+1)} \tag{5.7}$$

$$q^f = \frac{(\alpha - c^f - t) - n(1-\delta)(k^h - k^f)}{\beta(m+n+1)} \tag{5.8}$$

where $\partial q^h/\partial t < 0$, $\partial q^f/\partial t < 0$, $\partial q^h/\partial \delta > 0$, $\partial q^f/\partial \delta < 0$. Intuitively, an increase in the tax raises marginal costs and, consequently, output (foreign and home) falls. Home (foreign) firms' output rises (falls) with an increase in the local content, δ, because foreign firms become less cost competitive as they are required to employ less efficient inputs. The extent of the effect of the local content depends on the spread between k^h and k^f, that is, how inefficient home firms are vis-à-vis home firms. These results are consistent with the existing literature, for example, Lahiri and Ono (2004), Gautier (2017b).

Next, I shall characterize the welfare function of the government in the foreign country when there is no lobbying. I shall assume that the foreign country sets policy unilaterally and that the local content is determined exogenously. The government considers three components: (i) foreign firms repatriate profits, π^f, (ii) tax revenue arising from home firms, and (iii) consumer surplus since all the production is exported back to the foreign country. This set-up seeks to capture some of the key features of lobbying in the context of the relationship between the United States and Puerto Rico.

The foreign country's government welfare function when there is no lobbying is given by

$$W^f = CS(nq^h, mq^f) + ntq^h + m\pi^f \tag{5.9}$$

where CS denotes consumer surplus and ntq^h the tax revenue collected from home firms. It is noteworthy that in the absence of tax revenue from home firms, the optimal tax derived from (5.9) would be zero since in this way output, profits and consumer surplus are maximized. But because the government puts weight on the tax revenue collected from home firms the optimal tax is positive. Even though it will be apparent in the next section, it is noteworthy that this set-up allows to examine the case of interest here, which is that of a positive tax and how taxation is affected by lobbying.

THE POLITICAL EQUILIBRIUM

The previous section presented the model in the absence of any political contributions. This section follows Lahiri and Ono (2004, chapter 7) in the characterization of the equilibrium which arises from a two-stage game in the presence of political contributions. In the first stage foreign firms lobby the foreign country's government by choosing a political contribution schedule $\lambda(t)$, and in the second stage the government chooses the tax so as to maximize welfare taking the political contribution into consideration. That is,

$$\max_t V(t) = \rho\lambda(t) + W^f - \lambda(t) \tag{5.10}$$

where $\rho > 1$ is a constant which captures the weight the government puts on the political contribution and W^f is given by (5.9). Notice that if $\rho = 1$, then $V(\cdot) = W^f$ and therefore the government does not weigh lobbying by the foreign firms. The political contribution schedule, λ, is assumed to be a "truthful" equilibrium as defined in Dixit et al. (1997) and Lahiri and Ono (2004, 123). The contribution schedule assumes the following form

$$\lambda(t;z) = Max\{0, m\pi^f - z\} \tag{5.11}$$

where z denotes the reservation level of utility. A truthful equilibrium reflects the welfare effect of the policy (i.e., tax) in excess of the reservation level of utility. Given the contribution schedule $\lambda(t)$ in (5.11) the government maximizes (5.10) with respect to t which gives (subscripts denote derivatives):

$$\rho m\pi_t^f(t^*) + nq^h(t^*) + ntq_t^h(t^*) + CS(t^*) = 0 \tag{5.12}$$

where t^* is the level of the tax which maximizes (5.10).

The reservation level of utility, z, is determined by the following condition, which simply says that z is the maximum level of utility that the lobbying foreign firms can achieve given that the government would accept the contribution:

$$W^f(\tilde{t}) = W^f(t^*) + (\rho - 1)\lambda(t^*;z) \tag{5.13}$$

where $\tilde{t}$ denotes the tax that maximizes (5.9), that is, maximizes welfare in the absence of political contribution, and t^* is the level of the tax which maximizes welfare in the presence of political contribution. z is thus deter-mined from (5.13).[3]

COMPARATIVE STATICS

In this section I derive a few comparative statics results associated with the tax in the presence of lobbying. Using the condition in (5.12) and the closed-form solutions of the level of output, q^{h*}, q^{f*} in, respectively, (5.7) and (5.8), and therefore foreign profits, $\pi^f = \beta (q^{f*})^2$, gives the closed-form expression of the tax that maximizes welfare in the presence of political contribution:

$$t^* = \frac{m(m + n + 2\rho)\left(\alpha - c^f + n(1 - \delta)(k^h - k^f)\right) - n\left(\alpha - c^h - m(1 - \delta)(k^h - k^f)\right)}{m^2 - n^2 + 2(m\rho - n)}$$

(5.14)

where $t^* > 0$ as long as $m > n$. Notice that a positive tax holds even when the government puts no weight on political contributions, that is, at $\rho = 1$, $t^* = \tilde{t}$. Moreover, as ρ becomes very large t^* approaches $t^*_1 > 0$.[4] But interestingly, $t^*_1 \to 0$ as $\delta \to (\alpha - k^f)/(n - 1)(k^h - k^f)$. This result says that for sufficiently large local content the tax approaches zero as political contributions by for-eign firms become large.

Differentiation of (5.14) with respect to the level of political contribution gives

$$\frac{\mu^2}{2m} \frac{dt^*}{d\rho} = -(n^2 + m(n + 2) + 2)\left(\alpha - c^f + n(1 - \delta)(k^h - k^f)\right)$$

(5.15)

$$+ n\left(\alpha - c^h - m(1 - \delta)(k^h - k^f)\right) < 0 \text{ since } c^h > c^f$$

where $\mu = m^2 - n^2 + 2(m\rho - n)$. This result implies that as the weight the government puts on political contributions increases the equilibrium tax falls. This makes sense: with more weight on political contributions by foreign firms, the foreign government is more likely to lower the tax since a lower tax raises profits of foreign firms. Additionally, even in the case where home and foreign firms are almost equally efficient (i.e., $k^h \simeq k^f$) political contribu-tions reduce taxation. In this case the benefits from lower taxation are enjoyed equally by foreign and home firms since in this case both sets of firms exhibit the same level of cost-efficiency.

Proposition 1: *Let* m > n. *Then, the tax falls with increases in political con-tribution, that is, the tax is a decreasing function of political contributions.*

Proposition 2: *Even with very large political contributions the tax is not zero. However, if the local content is sufficiently large, then taxation approaches zero as political contributions become very large.*

Next, differentiation of (5.14) with respect to the local content gives

$$\mu \frac{dt^*}{d\delta} = -m(n + 1)\left(k^h - k^f\right)(m + n + 2\rho) - mn\left(k^h - k^f\right) < 0 \qquad (5.16)$$

where $\mu > 0$ since it is assumed that $m > n$. This result says that, for any level of political contribution, the tax falls as the local content increases. The reason is that with an increase in the local content profits of foreign firms fall and so the foreign government lowers the tax. Additionally, in (5.16) as political contributions increase the reduction in the tax becomes larger: this is because foreign firms look to offset the increase in the local content (which lowers their profits). The effects of the local content vanish as home and foreign firms become equally efficient, that is, $k^h \simeq k^f$ in which case the role of the local content becomes negligible since differences in cost competitiveness vanish.

Proposition 3: *For any level of political contribution, ρ, an increase in the local content, δ, lowers the tax, t*. The reduction in taxation, resulting from an increase in the local content, becomes larger as the level of political contribution rises.*

CONCLUDING REMARKS AND POLICY DISCUSSION

American firms play an important role in Puerto Rico's economy. To a large degree the reason American firms operate in Puerto Rico is because of unilaterally set policies by the US government. Given that lobbying plays an important role in policy setting, the study of potential lobbying by American firms seems relevant in the US-Puerto Rico case. The analysis indicates that policies to promote job growth in Puerto Rico via FDI (i.e., American firms) or increased political contributions by foreign firms is likely to result in a low-tax equilibrium. The foreign country has an incentive to set lower taxes in order to increase the flow of profits that goes back to the foreign country as well as consumer surplus. From an economic standpoint a lower tax should promote economic activity in Puerto Rico, but it also represents an equilibrium which is not consistent with statehood because under statehood taxes are likely to be relatively higher, *ceteris paribus*. Even though lower taxes benefit both sets of firms, it is more beneficial to foreign firms because these exhibit lower per-unit costs.

From a policy recommendation standpoint, the analysis suggests that without the ability to counteract the effects of political contributions a large share of the economic activity that takes place in Puerto Rico will flow back to the United States at the expense of Puerto Rico's economic development. In the context of the model presented here, however, one way to offset the effects of political contributions is, for example, to level any differences in efficiency between foreign and home firms. If home and foreign firms become equally efficient, then home firms may enjoy the benefits from political contributions without the expense of contributions. This is because lower taxation, resulting from political contribution, will benefit foreign and home firms equally. Therefore, from Puerto Rico's standpoint targeting cost-reducing policies, specifically to home firms vis-à-vis foreign firms, may be a way forward. Nonetheless, the extent to which this approach is at all possible depends upon whether the current US-Puerto Rico legal framework allows it (an aspect that touches on the issue of national sovereignty).

There are several potential extensions to the model. First, the model assumes that foreign firms are the only political contributors; extending the model to incorporate political contributions by both local (e.g., domestic firms lobbying to increase the local content) and foreign firms (i.e., lobbying for lower taxation as it is presented here) would allow to look at the interplay between lobbying objectives. However, in the context of the US-Puerto Rico political-economy relationship domestic (Puerto Rican) firms may be at a disadvantage vis-à-vis foreign (American) firms simply due to differences in resources available for lobbying and, therefore, in an extended model is likely to yield similar results to those presented here. Second, the present analysis assumes away the domestic country's welfare maximization problem, that is, optimally chosen local content. Allowing for the interplay between foreign and domestic governments' policymaking process, may yield interesting results. For instance, if the domestic government chooses the local content optimally and the foreign country then takes this policy as given and chooses the tax so as to maximize welfare, then the optimal tax could be smaller/larger than in the present analysis. This is because on the one hand a positive local content lowers foreign profits, thereby putting a downward pressure on the tax, but on the other the effects of the local content may well be very small thereby having a negligible effect on foreign profits. In this case a low-tax equilibrium arises but specifically via political contributions and not the local content. Third, the inclusion of product differentiation may play an important role in offsetting the effects on domestic firms. This is because with very differentiated products differences in cost competitive could be ameliorated.

NOTES

1. See draft of the "Puerto Rico Oversight, Management and Economic Stability Act."

2. If $k^h = k^f$ then $c^h = c^f$ and therefore δ vanishes from the marginal cost of foreign firms.

3. Lahiri and Ono (2004) rely on Grossman and Helpman (1994) to argue that z and λ are positive in equilibrium. I also shall rely on Lahiri and Ono's argument.

4. That is, using L'Hôpital's rule $t^* \rightarrow t^*_1 = \alpha - c^f + n(1 - \delta)(k^h - k^f) > 0$ as $\rho \rightarrow \infty$.

Chapter 6

Developing Domestic Industry and Jobs

The Role of the Local Content Requirement

There are an important number of countries which have used local content requirements across a myriad of industries to promote jobs and develop industry (UNIDO 1986, 2011a and 2011b; Sturgeon 1998; Ado 2013; UNCTAD 2014). For instance, Vietnam has regarded the local content, among others, as a way to develop domestic industries and promote forward and backward linkages in the domestic economy; specifically, the local content has been used in the motorbike and automobile manufacturing (UNIDO 2011a). More recently, UNCTAD (2014) discusses the use of the local content in the energy sector in a number of developed and less-developed countries. UNIDO (1986) shows evidence of a large share of developing countries which have used content requirements in the automobile industry during the 1980s, and several less-developed countries still use local content requirement policies in one way or another.[1]

In the case of Africa the analysis in UNIDO (2011b, 35–36) indicates that the establishment of foreign firms in the host country could increase their competitiveness by expanding the share of local content. Indeed, in strategic sectors, such as the oil, gas and mining sector, the local content has been used across a number of less-developed economies (Esteves, Coyne and Morone 2013). Other examples of countries which have used local content requirements are given in Lahiri and Ono (1998, 445). Given the potential role of the local content to promote jobs and increase efficiency in key sectors, it is surprising that such a policy tool has not been given more attention in the policy debate in Puerto Rico. This chapter seeks to feel this void.

The case of Puerto Rico, and specifically the establishment of US corporations in the pharmaceutical and chemicals sector, exemplifies the use of tax incentives to attract foreign firms, but with little impact on the development of forward and backward linkages (Dietz 2003). According to González

(1967), the industry which enjoys the tax benefits in Puerto Rico import the majority of the intermediate goods and exports a large part of its production back to the United States. Thus, the present analysis is motivated within the Puerto Rico-US case, as well as other less-developed economies, by specifically analyzing the role of the local content to promote domestic firms vis-à-vis foreign firms and potentially enhance linkages in the local economy.

To be fair, there are policies implemented by the Puerto Rican government which intend to promote local jobs via tax credits and technical aid to businesses, which somewhat capture the idea of the local content in terms of creating jobs and encouraging the development of local industries.[2] Nonetheless, the present analysis may aid in the understanding of the local content, specifically its potential to create jobs and promote the development of local industry.

The analysis indicates that there is an important role for the local content as a policy to develop local industry. Results are consistent with the literature, but are discussed in the context of the Puerto Rico-US case. The analysis shows that in the case of Puerto Rico there could be potentially important gains from the local content, but in order to achieve these Puerto Rico would need additional autonomy (i.e., national sovereignty) to implement such policy regime. The role of the local content is thus consistent with political independence for Puerto Rico, thus suggesting the need to move away from a statehood-like equilibrium. This is because the current regulatory framework restricts Puerto Rico's policymakers to set certain types of local content requirements due to potential inconsistencies with the Interstate Commerce Clause of the United States.[3] This Clause applies almost entirely to Puerto Rico. Thus, one of the policy implications of the present analysis is that more autonomy is needed to further develop the local industry and create jobs via local content requirements.

In terms of the existing theoretical literature, the framework of analysis fits into the analysis in Lahiri and Ono (2004), where a series of partial equilibrium models in the presence of local content requirement are presented. Lahiri and Ono (2004, 96, footnote 2) list a small literature on local content, none of which touches on the issue of the characteristics of optimal content requirement.[4] Lahiri and Ono (1998) consider a partial equilibrium model where policy consists of a local content requirement and profit taxation, local firms are fixed and foreign firms are endogenous, and the host country cares about employment.[5] They characterize the optimal profit tax and local content with respect to the number of domestic firms as well as efficiency levels, for example, they establish the conditions under which the host government may tax profits of foreign firms. In the present chapter I focus on the local content as the only policy available to the government in order to study its potential effects on welfare as well as the potential role of product differentiation on the optimal local content. The role of product differentiation with respect to the local content is explored to some extent and it is entirely new to the literature.

The model set-up consists of two sets of firms (foreign and home) which operate in the host (home) country and compete for the production of an imperfect substitute. The government in the home country commands foreign firms to employ a share of its resources from the local economy. I look at the case where the number of foreign firms is exogenous as well as endogenous. The analysis indicates, *inter alia*, that there is a positive local content which the local government can set consistent with welfare maximization, that is, there is a potential role for the local content. Additionally, I argue that as the local industry develops or differentiates itself from foreign competitors, the need to keep the local content diminishes. This result is important because it suggests that the local content could be used initially to develop industry, but it could be gradually phased out.

The rest of the chapter is structured as follows. The next section presents the model and key results both in the case where the number of foreign firms is exogenous and endogenous. The last section concludes.

THE LOCAL CONTENT REQUIREMENT: A MODEL

This section analyzes the case where domestic and foreign firms compete in the production of an imperfect substitute. Product differentiation is present in imperfectly competitive industries in Puerto Rico (e.g., pharmaceuticals and chemicals). Indeed, Ramcharran (2011, 402) argues that the pharmaceutical industry in Puerto Rico should allocate resources to the production of generic drugs (an imperfect substitute) to offset the phase out of the US federal tax credits schemes and increasing foreign competition. In the case of Vietnam local content has been used by the government in the automobile industry (an example of a differentiated product) and in other countries local content has also been implemented in the gas and oil industry (see Esteves, Coyne and Morone 2013).

The analysis indicates that, in line with the literature, there is a positive optimal local content under a number of cases. The policy implication for Puerto Rico is that stimulating local firms (via local content requirements) in the type of industry studied here raises domestic welfare. This suggests that there is no need to concentrate the entire industry on foreign firms. Second, in the case of the export-oriented firms, where consumer surplus effects are negligible, the analysis indicates an even stronger case for a local content. These policy recommendations are relevant because although it is in the interest of Puerto Rico to follow them, the extent to which the domestic government can implement a local content is largely limited by the US-Puerto Rico regulatory framework. The analysis thus points to the need for additional autonomy for policymakers in Puerto Rico to set policy. The analysis also indicates that even as domestic firms differentiate themselves, a case for the local content can be made. However, it is harder to make the case for the local content as the domestic industry matures in terms of the number of domestic firms operating in the host country, particularly when the number of foreign firms is exogenous.

To see these results I shall follow the model set-up in Lahiri and Ono (2004). Consider a host country in which a number m and n, respectively, of foreign and home (host) firms operate in the home country. I shall assume constant marginal costs c^h and c^f for the home and foreign firms, respectively, and therefore unit cost are equal to marginal cost. Home firms employ inputs from the home country, but foreign firms may use inputs from the domestic and foreign country. Let k^h and k^f denote, respectively, the marginal cost when production takes place using all inputs from the home and foreign country. I shall assume that foreign firms are relatively more cost efficient (i.e., $c^h > c^f$ *if and only if* $k^h > k^f$). Additionally, the government in the home country may command foreign firms to employ a share, δ, of domestic inputs. Therefore, marginal costs for the home and foreign firms are given by

$$c^h = k^h \tag{6.1}$$

$$c^f = (1 - \delta)k^f + \delta k^h \tag{6.2}$$

Each home firm i ($i = 1,2, \dots, n$) and foreign firm j ($j = 1,2, \dots, m$) compete for the production of an imperfect substitute and choose the level of output in a Cournot-Nash fashion. In particular, foreign and home firms solve

$$\max_{q_i^h} \pi_i^h = (p - c^h)q_i^h - F^h \tag{6.3}$$

$$\max_{q_j^f} \pi_j^f = (p - c^f)q_j^f - F^f \tag{6.4}$$

where F^z denotes fixed costs for each firm in country $z = h, f$. Consider a demand structure where horizontal product differentiation is present. In particular, demand comes from preferences such that

$$p^h = \alpha - \beta(q_1^h + \cdots + q_n^h) - \gamma(q_1^f + \cdots + q_m^f) \tag{6.5}$$

$$p^f = \alpha - \beta(q_1^f + \cdots + q_m^f) - \gamma(q_1^h + \cdots + q_n^h) \tag{6.6}$$

where $\beta > \gamma > 0$ and γ denotes the degree of product differentiation. This type of demand structure has been used in Lahiri and Symeonidis (2007) and Gautier (2013, 2014, 2017). I shall assume for now that the number of foreign and domestic firms is fixed. Solving (6.3) and (6.4) yields under symmetry the following two first-order conditions

$$p - c^h = \beta q^h \tag{6.7}$$

$$p - c^f = \beta q^f \tag{6.8}$$

where $p^h = \alpha - \beta n q^h - \gamma m q^f$, $p^f = \alpha - \beta m q^f - \gamma n q^h$. From (6.7) and (6.8) the symmetric Cournot-Nash levels of output for foreign firms, $\bar{q}^f$, and home firms, $\bar{q}^h$, are given by

$$\omega \bar{q}^h = \beta(m+1)(\alpha - c^h) - m\gamma(\alpha - c^f) \Rightarrow \omega \frac{\partial \bar{q}^h}{\partial \delta} = \gamma m(k^h - k^f) \tag{6.9}$$

$$\omega \bar{q}^f = \beta(n+1)(\alpha - c^f) - n\gamma(\alpha - c^h) \Rightarrow \omega \frac{\partial \bar{q}^f}{\partial \delta} = -\beta(n+1)(k^h - k^f) \tag{6.10}$$

$$p^h = \alpha - n\beta \bar{q}^h - m\gamma \bar{q}^f \Rightarrow \omega \frac{\partial p^h}{\partial \delta} = \beta \gamma m(k^h - k^f) \tag{6.11}$$

where $k^h > k^f$ and $\omega = \beta^2(m+1)(n+1) - nm\gamma^2 > 0$ from the stability conditions of the Cournot equilibrium (Dixit 1986). The effect of the local content requirement is to stimulate home firms at the expense of foreign firms (see expressions of partial derivatives). This is because by assumption foreign firms are relatively more cost efficient. It is noteworthy that industry output, $nq^h + mq^f$, falls with an increase in the content requirement. This is because an increase in the local content induces less production by the more efficient foreign firms.

The government in the home country solves

$$\max_{\delta} = W^h = CS^h(nq^h, mq^f) + n\pi^h + nq^h k^h + mq^f k^h \delta \tag{6.12}$$

where, as in Lahiri and Ono (1998), the cost of using domestic inputs by foreign firms enters as income into the welfare function of the host country, that is, $nq^h k^h + mq^f k^h \delta$. In particular, differentiation of the welfare function (6.12) gives

$$\frac{\partial W^h}{\partial \delta} = mq^f \left(k^h - \frac{\partial p^f}{\partial \delta} \right) + np^h \frac{\partial q^h}{\partial \delta} + \delta mk^h \frac{\partial q^f}{\partial \delta} \tag{6.13}$$

where $k^h - \partial p^f/\partial\delta > 0$, and at $\delta = 0$, $\partial W^h/\partial\delta > 0$. Setting (6.13) equal to zero (subscripts denote partial derivatives) the optimal content then must satisfy

$$\bar{\delta} = \frac{-nq_\delta^h p^h - mk^h q^f + mq^f p_\delta^f}{mk^h q_\delta^f} > 0 \qquad (6.14)$$

where $q^h_\delta > 0$, $q^f_\delta < 0$ and $p^f_\delta > 0$.[6] The expression in (6.14) says that there are three effects at play, which the government in the home country has to balance. The first and second terms are, respectively, the profit and income effects, which are positive. This suggests that the government stimulates profits and income (and thus raises welfare) with the content requirement. In contrast, the third term, the price effect, is negative which suggests that the government lowers the content requirement to increase output thus lowering prices and increasing welfare.

The expression in (6.14) points to the existence of a positive optimal content requirement, which is less than one, for a range of n.[7] The existence of such policy also holds in the extreme cases of very differentiated products ($\gamma \simeq 0$) and when goods are nearly homogeneous ($\gamma \simeq \beta$).

Proposition 1: *In the case where the number of foreign and domestic firms is exogenous, for a range of* n *there exists an optimal content requirement for any degree of product differentiation.*

Proposition 1 has several policy implications. First, in the presence of consumer surplus there is a negative welfare effect arising from the content requirement (equilibrium industry output falls and the price rises), but this negative welfare effect is completely offset by the increase in income arising from the content requirement. Thus, even in the presence of consumer surplus effects there is a potential role for the local content requirement when employment is an important part of the welfare analysis. Second, in the case where consumer surplus effects are relatively small and the number of domestic firms operating in the host country is negligible, the analysis indicates the important role of the content requirement in generating employment in the host country. This result also holds in the case (as we shall see later) where foreign firms can exit the market and establish operations elsewhere. Third, in the case where consumer surplus effects are relatively small a positive content requirement reduces output by foreign firms operating in the home country and raises output by home firms; that is, home firms capture a larger share of the market arising from lower output by foreign firms. As a result, profits in the home country and income rise (positive welfare effects) thus offsetting any reductions in output by foreign firms operating in the home country. Thus, even with the reduction in foreign firms' output the local content requirement can still play a role because of the positive welfare effects it generates via higher profits of domestic firms. Fourth, if employment effects are relatively small (so consumer surplus and domestic profits are key), then the existence of an optimal content requirement still holds. This is because the welfare reduction in consumer surplus is completely offset by the increase in the profits of domestic firms.

A key aspect in the analysis is that profits of foreign firms are assumed away. This assumption is consistent with the issue at hand here (i.e., foreign American firms operating in Puerto Rico) where profits are repatriated or very little stays in the local economy as in the case of large US retailers.

Next, I touch on the issue of how the number of domestic firms affects the optimal content requirement. In particular, I want to answer the question as to whether the government should keep offering the local content requirement even in the presence of a large number of domestic firms. The presence of a large number of domestic firms may suggest that the local industry has developed sufficiently (at least in size, but not necessarily improved in terms of efficiency) so that it no longer needs the local content requirement to develop the industry further. The case where the number of foreign firms is endogenous is considered below so the issue as to whether domestic firms force foreign firms to exit the market is assumed away for now. Additionally, recall that I conduct the analysis under the assumption that domestic firms exhibit higher unit costs relative to their foreign counterparts. The analysis indicates that the optimal content requirement may rise or fall with an increase in the number of domestic firms and this effect is negligible as products become very differentiated, that is, $\gamma \simeq 0$.

To see this, total differentiation of $W^h_{\delta}(\bar{\delta}(n), n)$ yields (see Appendix B to this chapter for a derivation)

$$
\left(-\frac{W^h_{\delta\delta}\omega^2}{m\beta}\right)\bar{\delta}_n = \left(k^h - k^f\right)\gamma\left[\beta(m+1)\left(p^h - nq^h\beta\right) + \beta mnq^h\gamma^2\right]
$$
$$
-\gamma\left[q^h\left(k^h\beta^2(n+1) + mk^f\left(\beta^2(n+1) - n\gamma^2\right)\right) + \left(k^h - k^f\right)\gamma\left(-q^f\beta + \delta k^h m\right)\right]
$$
$$(6.15)$$

where $W^h_{\delta\delta} < 0$ (subscripts denote partial derivatives) because of the concavity of the welfare function, and $-q^f\beta + \delta k^h m > 0$, $p^h - nq^h\beta > 0$.

The first term in Equation (6.15) is the profit effect, which is positive, and the second the income and price effects, which are negative. The sign of (6.15) is therefore ambiguous. Intuitively, an increase in the number of domestic firms lowers profits (each domestic firm's profits) and, as a result, the government offsets this effect by increasing the content requirement in order to stimulate home output and raise profits. On the other hand, an increase in n lowers output by foreign firms, and so income falls and the price faced by foreign firms rises. As a result, the government reacts by reducing the content requirement in order to stimulate production by foreign firms (a reduction in the local content lowers the marginal cost of foreign firms). In the special case where products are completely differentiated ($\gamma \simeq 0$) the effect of a change in the number of firms is negligible. This is because with completely differentiated products differences in cost competitiveness between foreign and domestic firms become small and, consequently, the government cannot offset the increase in the number of domestic firms through the local content requirement.

The ambiguous sign of (6.15) raises the question as to whether further increases in the number of home firms drives the optimal content to zero. Inspection of $\bar{\delta}$ indicates that, in effect, as n becomes very large the optimal content becomes small. This is because a large n drives down output by home firms and profits, but raises output by foreign more efficient firms, thereby raising income and consumer surplus via lower prices. The need for a local content therefore becomes small. One policy implication here is that, for any given level of relative efficiency between foreign and home firms, a sufficiently large number of domestic firms induce the government to set a very small content requirement.

Proposition 2: *In the case where the number of foreign firms is exogenous, a sufficiently large number of home firms results in a small optimal content requirement.*

Next, I consider the case where foreign firms can exit the market in which they operate if profits fall below a given threshold; the free-entry condition is thus captured by $\pi^f = \tilde{\pi}^f$. The idea here is to look at one of the arguments against the imposition of the local content requirement, namely, that it may induce foreign firms to leave the home country market and establish operations elsewhere. It is shown, *inter alia*, that in the case where $k^h > k^f$ the optimal content is positive, a result which suggests that even in the presence of competition from domestic firms and free entry and exit of foreign firms, the domestic government has an incentive to adopt a local content requirement.

The profit-maximizing first-order conditions and the free-entry condition yields

$$\beta(\breve{q}^f)^2 = F + \tilde{\pi}^f ; (\beta^2(n+1) - n\gamma^2)\breve{q}^h = (\alpha - c^h)\beta - \gamma(\alpha - c^f) + \gamma\beta\breve{q}^f$$
$$(6.16)$$

$$\breve{q}^f(\beta^2(n+1) - n\gamma^2)\breve{m} = (\alpha - c^f)\beta(n+1) - (\alpha - c^h)n\gamma - \beta^2(n+1)\breve{q}^f$$
$$(6.17)$$

The effect of the content requirement on m and p^f is given by

$$m_\delta = \frac{-\beta(k^h - k^f)(n+1)}{q^f(\beta^2(n+1) - \gamma^2 n)} < 0; \quad q_\delta^h = \frac{\gamma(k^h - k^f)}{\beta^2(n+1) - \gamma^2 n} > 0; \quad p_\delta^f = (k^h - k^f) > 0$$

(6.18)

In order to analyze optimal policy when m is endogenous the government solves (6.12) which yields

$$\frac{\partial W^h}{\partial \delta} = np^h \frac{\partial q^h}{\partial \delta} - mq^f \frac{\partial p^f}{\partial \delta} + mq^f k^h + q^f k^h \delta \frac{\partial m}{\partial \delta} \Rightarrow \left. \frac{\partial W^h}{\partial \delta} \right|_{\delta=0} > 0 \Rightarrow \delta > 0$$

(6.19)

In other words, the optimal policy, $\breve{\delta}$ is positive, where from the government's first-order condition one obtains

$$\breve{\delta} = \frac{-nq_\delta^h p^h - mk^h q^f + mq^f p_\delta^f}{mk^h q^f m_\delta} > 0$$

(6.20)

As before there are three effects at play, namely, the profit and income effects (the first two terms which push upwards the optimal local content requirement), and the price effect (the third term) which pushes downwards the policy. In contrast to the case where m is exogenous, changes in foreign output takes place via changes in the number of foreign firms. It is noteworthy that the main policy implication here is that the local content requirement has a role to play even when foreign firms can exit the market. The closed-form expression for the optimal content requirement is given by

$$\breve{\delta} = \frac{\beta k^f(\alpha + nk^h - k^f(n+1))/(k^h - k^f) + \breve{q}^f \gamma \left(n\gamma - \frac{\beta(n+1)k^f}{k^h - k^f}\right) + nk^f \gamma}{k^f(\gamma n + \beta(n+1)) - k^h(\gamma n - \beta(n+1))} > 0$$

(6.21)

where $\alpha - k^f + n(k^h - k^f) > 0$. Since the optimal policy is always positive, for an interior solution one requires

$$\breve{\delta} < 1 \Leftrightarrow n < n_1 = \frac{\beta(k^{h^2} - (\alpha - \gamma q^f)k^f)}{q^f \gamma(\gamma k^h - k^f(\beta + \gamma)) - k^h(\beta - \gamma(k^h - k^f))}$$

(6.22)

where $0 < n_1$.[8] As long as $0 < n < n_1$, policy gets close to one as the number of firms approaches n_1. This is because a large n lowers profits and output by domestic firms, which also results in an increase in the output of foreign firms. In addition, foreign firms enter the market and, as a result, the government raises the content requirement to control for the number (entry) of foreign firms. However, policy does not approach zero in the case where $n \simeq 0$. This is because even with little competition from domestic firms the government can raise income from foreign firms by setting a positive content requirement. In this case few domestic competitors result in a large increase in employment (output) by foreign firms and so imposing the local requirement on foreign firms raises welfare due to the large market share these firms have.

Proposition 3: *In the case where the number of foreign firms is endogenous, for a given range of* n, *there exists an optimal local content requirement for any degree of product differentiation. Furthermore, a sufficiently large number of home firms,* n, *results in a relatively large local content to control for the excessive entry of foreign firms.*

The analysis underscores the role of free entry: in the case where the number of foreign firms is endogenous (exogenous) an increase in the number of home firms induces an increase (decrease) in the optimal local content requirement.

CONCLUSION

The analysis presents a partial equilibrium model of foreign direct investment to analyze the potential role of a local content requirement in the presence of product differentiation both in the case where the number of foreign firms is exogenous and endogenous. The model intends to capture features specific to the US-Puerto Rico relationship, for example, imperfectly competitive markets in the chemicals and manufacturing sectors where American firms have played a prominent role in Puerto Rico's economy in terms of job creation. The analysis indicates that there is a role for the local content to develop industry and create jobs, particularly in the case where the number of home firms is small and in the free-entry case. The role of the local content seems relevant for any degree of product differentiation. It is noteworthy that in the case where products are very differentiated and the number of firms is fixed, adjustments in the local content, resulting from changes in the number of local firms, vanish. The implication here is that if industry in Puerto Rico differentiates itself sufficiently from foreign competition, then the role of the local content becomes negligible as industry matures.

In any case, in the context of the local content there are regulatory constraints arising from the political relationship between the United States and Puerto Rico. In other words, even though it would be potentially beneficial to employ a local content requirement to boost industry and jobs, this may not be entirely feasible from a regulatory practical standpoint. Therefore, if a policy like this is to be used, then more autonomy by policymakers in Puerto Rico would be needed.

There are areas for future research which could be explored in the present model set-up, including a deeper analysis of the relationship between the degree of product differentiation and the optimal local content. This line of research could offer further insights into the analysis of industries characterized by product differentiation, for example, the production of generic drugs. Additionally, in order to capture more explicitly the US-Puerto Rico relationship political aspects could be modeled via, for example, incorporating a tax into the model (the role of such a tax is modeled in chapter 3). This would capture the interaction between the two economies and, at the same time, provide a richer framework where taxes play a role via marginal costs.

NOTES

1. See Esteves, Coyne and Morone (2013), appendix A.

2. For example, Act 120 of 2014, "Ley de Incentivos para la Generación y Retención de Empleos en las PyMEs," and Act 14 of 2014, "Investment Act for the Puerto Rican Industry (JIIP)," and Asociación de Productos Hechos en Puerto Rico seek to promote and protect industries based in Puerto Rico.

3. For example, the no-longer-in-place protective regulation in the beer industry which required all bottled beer to be in dark glass.

4. On a different strand of the literature Qiu and Tao (2001) look at the content requirement in the context of heterogeneous multinational firms.

5. Lahiri and Ono (2004) consider a similar setting in a two-country general equilibrium framework.

6. See appendix B for the expression of $\bar{\delta}$.

7. The closed-form solution for the optimal local content requirement in the case where the number of firms is exogenous yields a function $\bar{\delta}(n)$. Then, imposing the condition $\bar{\delta}(n) < 1$ gives a polynomial of degree two in n. I shall assume that there is at least a positive root, greater than one.

8. For the non-negativity assumption of $n1$ the following conditions are imposed. If $k^h \gamma - k^f (\beta + \gamma) < 0$, then one needs $k^{h2} - (\alpha - \gamma q^f) k^f < 0$ so that $n_1 > 0$. From the non-negativity assumption of m, $\alpha - k^f - \gamma q^f > 0$ and therefore $\alpha - \gamma q^f > 0$. It is noteworthy that $k^h \gamma n - k^f (\beta(n+1) + n\gamma) < 0$ in order to be consistent with $k^h\gamma - k^f (\beta + \gamma) < 0$. Additionally, note that at $n = 0$, $\bar{\delta} > 0$.

Chapter 7

Income Convergence and Sustained Growth

A Comment

One of the arguments often times put forward by pro-statehood movements is that Puerto Rico's economy, as a fully incorporated state of the United States, will experience an increase in economic activity, income and, consequently, a convergence in income with other states of the United States. This would imply, in turn, an unambiguous improvement in the standard of living in Puerto Rico. In this chapter I examine (and challenge) this line of reasoning from a purely economic standpoint.

In particular, I survey the empirical literature to see if (i) there is evidence to suggest that Puerto Rico's economy is likely to converge with the US economy should Puerto Rico become the fifty-first state of the United States and (ii) whether there is evidence to suggest that more participation in the US political arena translates into *sustained* long-run growth for Puerto Rico. The analysis suggests that there is not strong evidence for either (i) or (ii). The policy implication here is, therefore, that to achieve *sustained* long-run growth Puerto Rico's economy should focus on the implementation of trade-oriented policies rather than relying on additional aid from the US federal government. Additionally, I propose (as many have) that, based on past experience in US policymaking, the transition to a more trade-oriented equilibrium should be a gradual one in order to allow for an adequate re-allocation of resources conducive to attracting capital and, consequently, putting Puerto Rico's economy back on a path to recovery.

There are a number of important recent empirical studies which indicate that there is evidence to suggest that states in the United States exhibited converge until the 1980s, but over the last 30 years the evidence suggests otherwise (e.g., Ganong and Shoag 2012; Breuer, Hauk and McDermott 2014; Holmes, Otero and Panagiotidis 2014; Choi and Wang 2015).[1] Thus, even though statehood may induce a short-run increase in income via a relatively small net increase in federal funds (GAO 2014), the evidence thus far does not suggest convergence (e.g., ECLAC 2004; Luciano 2014).[2] Additionally, in general within-state income shares for the top 1 percent (including capital gains) have increased at a rapid pace, a trend which is also present for the United States as a country (see Alvaredo et al. (2013) for a brief discussion and Alvaredo et al., "The world wealth and income database," http://www. wid.world/ for state-level data).

The importance of the results in Ganong and Shoag (2012), as well as other empirical studies in the literature, is that they suggest non-convergence in income in the long-run should Puerto Rico join the United States as its fifty-first state. In Ganong and Shoag's study one of the key channels whereby converge might take place is the flow of labor across states; however, this flow of labor (skilled and unskilled) has not been sufficient over the last 30 years to yield income convergence. In the case of Puerto Rico, we have not seen strong evidence of convergence, even when labor can move freely and legally across Puerto Rico and the United States. Factors such as culture, language, and skill sets may help explain the lack of labor flow, but further research in this area is needed.

Furthermore, the works by Holmes, Otero and Panagiotidis (2014), and Choi and Wang (2015) suggest that differences in initial income, as well as differences in technology levels and human capital, play a key role in explaining the degree of non-convergence exhibited among US states. This result is important because (i) it suggests that technological diffusion may not take place across US states in a frictionless fashion (i.e., statehood for Puerto Rico would still exhibit costs associated to access technology in the United States) and (ii) importantly large differences in income are associated with a smaller degree of convergence (this is important given Puerto Rico's low level of income).

What are then some of the economic mechanisms whereby we could expect convergence under statehood for Puerto Rico? As mentioned earlier, one possibility is a relatively small potential increase in net federal funds, but this arguably would be too small to explain any convergence (GAO [2014] estimates in about $5 billion the net influx of federal funds). Additionally, based on current data the structure of federal welfare programs does not seem to be stimulating job creation or improving productivity (Krueger, Teja and Wolfe 2015). A second potential mechanism would be that as a state Puerto Rico would experience "positive" business expectations thereby helping the economy via less uncertainty. However, given the evidence of non-convergence across US states it is hard to make the case for convergence based on uncertainty alone. In fact, issues of uncertainty may be addressed via credible policies either under a statehood or non-statehood equilibrium. In other words, impediments to growth for the Puerto Rican economy resulting specifically from uncertainty can be effectively addressed either under a statehood or non-statehood scenario. This analysis is in line with Lara (2014).

Luciano (2014, 29) argues that there are four important economy-related variables which may change as a result of statehood, for example, type of institutions, policies associated with subsidies and taxes, size of government, economic policy.[3] The author argues these variables represent a small share of the total number of variables presented in the literature which may induce convergence in the case of Puerto Rico. As a result, statehood is likely to bring, via the aforementioned variables, insufficient growth so as to achieve convergence, particularly as it pertains to trade-induced growth. Partly this is because changes in these variables are likely to exhibit marginal changes in a statehood equilibrium, except perhaps in parity of federal aid programs and taxation. But as previously discussed data suggest that *sustained* long-run growth for Puerto Rico is not likely to hold via additional aid from the US federal government.

To this discussion it is important to mention political participation. In particular, to what extent does having a political say in US policymaking may help take Puerto Rico to a convergence path? There are at least two points worth mentioning about this. On the one hand, greater participation via political representation in the US Congress (Senate and House) may increase the probability of access to federal programs and funding to boost growth (with a potentially negative effect on productivity levels in Puerto Rico); but on the other, the experience of low-income states (e.g., Mississippi, Arkansas) does not seem to support the claim that more participation implies high growth and thus convergence. In other words, having a "seat" at the "negotiating table" does not necessarily translate into income growth and convergence. Indeed, the empirical literature does not present strong evidence to suggest that simply political access ensures growth and/or access to additional federal spending (e.g., Levitt and Poterba 1999; Knight 2005).

In an important empirical paper, Levitt and Poterba (1999) present, using panel data from 1953 to 1990, convincing evidence which suggests that there is a link between political participation and economic outcomes; but specifically a link between "very senior" and "influential" House representatives and state-level economic growth as measured by GSP and income levels.[4] The allocation of federal spending, however, is not systematically correlated with seniority or committee membership, a result consistent with the literature according to Hoover and Pecorino (2005). Thus, the connection between political participation and growth is not clear-cut.

On federal spending for smaller states, the literature suggests (Atlas et al. 1995; Hoover and Pecorino 2005; Knight 2008) that although federal spending in some categories in relatively smaller states is associated with senate representation (albeit not house representation), additional federal spending does not necessarily translate into higher growth rates (Horthváth, Moore and Rork 2014). Specifically, there is an overall (very small) positive effect on growth rates (just over a 0.20 percentage point increase in growth rates) resulting from federal spending, with potentially negative impacts on growth rates from programs which alleviate poverty. This simply illustrates the point made earlier: more federal spending does not imply higher *sustained* income growth, particularly via federal spending which does not target productivity-enhancing programs. Indeed, the focus of policy should be, via international trade in the case of Puerto Rico, on encouraging labor productivity via human capital, infrastructure improvements and a diversified industrial mix, all of which are determinants of long-run growth for US states as indicated in the literature (see Atems (2015), and Carlino and Voith (1992) as examples in the literature).

In the case of Puerto Rico the key implication from the aforementioned literature is that sufficiently large growth rates, so as to achieve convergence, are not likely to take place via additional federal spending and/or political participation; this is because of the relatively small impact on *sustained* growth. Additionally, the experience of low-income states is that, although they have enjoyed an increase in growth rates as a result of political variables, these growth rates are not likely to be sufficiently large to achieve convergence (see table 4, Levitt and Poterba 1999). To be fair, as a newly admitted state Puerto Rico would likely enjoy parity in many federal spending programs, thereby encouraging economic activity in the short run but not necessarily in *a sustained* fashion.

Figure C.8 raises questions about whether there is evidence for convergence between Puerto Rico and a selected number of low-income US states, for example, Mississippi. According to the figure, Puerto Rico's economy would need to grow, *ceteris paribus*, at a very rapid rate in order to catch up with other states. Indeed, historical data show that even during periods of rapid growth Puerto Rico has not been able to achieve the level of *sustained* growth needed to catch up. The policy recommendation here is, therefore, that any change in growth-enhancing factors should oscillate around the implementation of trade-promoting policies, a relatively costly economic policy framework under statehood (see chapter 2). The reasoning here is that trade-promoting policies will allow capital to flow into Puerto Rico's economy thereby raising factor productivities and consequently economic growth.

It is noteworthy that the cases of the states of Hawaii and Alaska are often times offered as examples of states whose incomes' converged with that of the US-wide economy after becoming a state of the union. Relying on these examples assumes away several important aspects, that is, it assumes away the driving forces which may have led to convergence. Certainly, military spending and tourism were two dominant factors which led to income growth in Hawaii. And military spending to this day arguably still plays an important role in the Hawaiian economy. Moreover, the development of the jet engine also reduced transportation costs, and growing incomes in Japan and United States boosted tourism in Hawaii. The Korean and Vietnam wars boosted military spending and growth; the Second World War boosted growth pre-1945. Additionally, sugar production seemed to have contributed significantly to the Hawaiian economy, possibly driven by protectionist policies to the sugar industry implemented by the United States as well as market conditions at the time.

Can we expect military spending and tourism to drive Puerto Rico's economy if it becomes a state of the United States? To answer this question it is noteworthy that, first, military spending has arguably declined consistently over the years in Puerto Rico and there is no evidence to indicate that it will increase significantly in the future. The global geopolitical arena is gravitating toward Asia and the Middle East, and thus resources will be allocated accordingly by US policymakers. Moreover, growth in the tourism industry in Puerto Rico may rise because of rising incomes elsewhere, that is, the demand for tourism in Puerto Rico may raise as a result of higher incomes in the United States and other high-income countries. Interestingly, a statehood equilibrium for Puerto Rico may provide a boost to the tourism industry as a result of other sectors in the economy shrinking. But does Puerto Rico want to rely on an economy based on tourism? This is the case which Baumol (2007) calls the tourism trap. I believe that relying on tourism as the key engine for growth may not necessarily be the best approach to growth policy.

The comparison with Hawaii does not make a strong case for convergence, which is line with more recent evidence.[5] And in the case of Alaska income convergence was arguably driven primarily by factor endowments (e.g., oil industry) in that state; factor endowments in Alaska are certainly very different from those Puerto Rico enjoys.

Stiglitz (2012) describes in a detailed and clear fashion the growing economic and social inequality in the United States. The author argues, convincingly, that there is increasingly a gap between income and wealth. Additionally, the author talks about the deterioration of real salaries of the middle class and low-income households, but at the same time there has been a large increase in salaries and wealth of high-income households. One of the challenges with the rising income and wealth gap is that it undermines the ability of low-income households to move up the income ladder. In part this is because of the lack of access to quality education of low-income households, whereas high-income households have relatively more access to quality education. Stiglitz (2012, 25) enumerates some of the consequences of a rising inequality, namely, the myth of the American dream and the rising inequality vis-à-vis other industrialized countries.

These results present a less than desirable picture for the prospects of Puerto Rico becoming a state and the consequences to Puerto Rico as a state. This is because for a low-income, low-growth economy (i) rising inequality would deteriorate the prospects for growth and development and (ii) would create further costs to the US federal government in welfare spending programs (GAO 2014).

It is noteworthy that social and economic inequality may pose impediments to long-run economic growth. This is because the lack of access to quality education, access to affordable quality medical care, and the potential social and political instability arising from inequality yields inefficiencies in the economy, among others. Sotomayor (2004) shows that income inequality in Puerto Rico exhibited an upward trend in the 1990s while the economy grew during that period. Segarra (2006) argues that inequality is exacerbated during periods of slow economic activity in Puerto Rico, where low-income households are the most affected. With these in mind, if income inequality is rising in the United States and Puerto Rico, and income inequality retards long-run growth, then one may conjecture that for Puerto Rico to join the United States as a state of the union would not result in a reduction in long-run income inequality and better long-run economic prospects. It is true that there is evidence of the offsetting effects of US transfers on income inequality and poverty in Puerto Rico (Sotomayor 2004), but the rising trend in income inequality in Puerto Rico still persisted in the 1990s, a period of strong economic growth for the United States and Puerto Rico. Therefore, in terms of reducing income inequality in Puerto Rico the present political and economic relationship with the United States (including the present regulatory framework) has not been sufficiently strong to achieve a sufficient reduction in inequality, and at the same time *sustained* growth in Puerto Rico. A different policy approach to promote *sustained* long-run growth and development is thus warranted.

In the case of Puerto Rico, one of the ways to tackle rising income inequality would be to restore economic growth. As argued in chapter 2, in order to put Puerto Rico on a sustainable growth path its economy needs to be inserted into the global economy, thereby providing business opportunities for local entrepreneurs, increasing economic efficiency, and lowering prices to consumers and businesses. These may be efficiently achieved through a higher degree of autonomy for Puerto Rican policymakers. This is because the key economic variables to insert Puerto Rico's economy into the global economy are controlled unilaterally by US policymakers and, therefore, set to benefit the US economy which, in effect, enjoys a very different economic profile in terms of its regulatory framework and factor endowments vis-à-vis Puerto Rico.

An active participation in global markets would surely enable the re-allocation of resources in Puerto Rico to tackle income inequality and thus enhance growth prospects. And the path to achieving the insertion into global markets requires close coordination between United States and Puerto Rico's policy-makers. The implementation of this transition should be done in a gradual and credible fashion. Indeed, there are historical examples which illustrate that there is a precedent in this area of policy (Duprey-Selgado 2016) thus facilitating the implementation of such transition for Puerto Rico and the United States. A gradual transition to a substantially more open economy, with a larger degree of participation in global markets, will put in motion a set of credible policies to restore growth. In turn these policies would likely help Puerto Rico to address efficiently its short-run fiscal constraints as well as improve its chances to achieve sustained growth.

NOTES

1. http://dash.harvard.edu/handle/1/9361381

2. http://bibliotecasoberanista.files.wordpress.com/2014/05/capc3adtulo-6-el-debate-sobre-la-estadidad-como-vehc3adculo-de-convergencia-en-crecimiento-econ-c3b3mico.pdf. To be fair, according to Luciano (2014, 13) a study by ECLAC shows evidence of convergence between the United States and Puerto Rico in the following periods: 1947–1971 and 1986–2002, but divergence in the following period: 1971–1986.

3. There is a large empirical literature which examines the extent to which these factors are growth-enhancing. Results on long- and short-run impacts depend upon variables measurement, model specification, among others. For a brief discussion on some of the literature see example, Wink and Eller (1998), Horthváth, Moore and Rork (2014).

4. Levitt and Poterba (1999, 186) state that "In spite of these effects of political variables on economic growth rates, we find no consistent association between political variables and the allocation of federal spending, leaving us without a convincing explanation of the correlation between political variables and economic growth."

5. See http://forbes.house.gov/uploadedfiles/bloomberg.pdf; http://eh.net/ency-clopedia/economic-history-of-hawaii/; http://www.rand.org/pubs/technical reports/TR996.html

Chapter 8

Market-based Environmental Policy in Puerto Rico

MARKET-BASED MECHANISMS: A REVIEW OF POLICY EFFORTS

This section describes some of the efforts put forward by policymakers in Puerto Rico to establish market-based policies to address air pollution in that country.[1] In addition, preliminary regression analysis is presented which indicates that there is a potential role for carbon-pricing policies in Puerto Rico. The goal of this chapter is thus to understand the current situation of environmental policy in Puerto Rico, in particular market-based policies, in order to make policy recommendations. In a sense this section may serve as a literature review of current policymaking in the context of environmental policy in Puerto Rico. Various sources of information were used in the analysis; in particular, the literature review relies on current legislation (i.e., current laws), graduate work (e.g., dissertations and theses) at the University of Puerto Rico and Inter-American University of Puerto Rico, books and analyses written by scholars which are mainly available at different repository institutions across the country.

The main results from the analysis are that very little has been done to put a price on carbon (e.g., air pollution) via a cap and trade system and/or an emission tax, two important market-based mechanisms, and that efficiency gains are indeed possible via the development of regional markets. Nevertheless, there are numerous examples of incentives of subsidies to promote renewable technologies (see e.g., Energy Cluster's website and Irizarry-Mora (2012) for examples), and the literature review suggests the use of contingent valuation methods to estimate willingness to pay for environmental resources (rainforest visits) by local and international tourists (e.g., Loomis and Santiago 2009, 2011) and beaches (Loomis and Santiago 2013). The latter is a line of research to build from in order to estimate potential environmental fees. Moreover, I argue that in order to achieve market efficiency gains from a regional market-based policy framework, and in line with an equilibrium consistent with national sovereignty (i.e., political independence), further autonomy in the policymaking arena may be needed. In the remaining of this section a brief description of some of these efforts is presented.

Environmental challenges are not new to Puerto Rico and the trade-off between development and environmental quality has been identified in the literature (Concepción 2000). Irizarry-Mora (2012) describes the increasing contribution of Puerto Rico to global emissions as well as the energy needs in the context of Puerto Rico's economy. The *Puerto Rico Climate Change Council* and *Puerto Rico 2025*, the latter a study conducted by the consulting firm A.T. Kearney in 2003, identify some of the challenges and strengths of Puerto Rico in the context of environmental policy. Some of the challenges include rising ocean temperatures, frequency of tropical storms, lack of recycling programs and environmental consciousness, and very little compliance of environmental policies, the latter being particularly an important challenge.

On the other hand, some of the strengths include potential growth for ecotourism, particularly given the natural endowment of the country, and a well-established legal and regulatory framework. Concepción (1990) describes some of the challenges faced by policymakers to develop sustainable economic policies and analyzes the impact of development policy approach on environmental policy. The author shows evidence which suggests that the incentives to develop capital-intensive and possibly pollution-intensive industries have been implemented at the expense of lesser environmental regulation. Interestingly, the author notes that employment problems persist (at the expense of environmental degradation) and economic growth has not been consistent. Seguinot-Barbosa (2011) describes the process through which the environmental impact of development projects is analyzed by policymakers; this illustrates one potential regulatory process whereby environmental degradation may be prevented.

The legal and regulatory framework to environmental policy in Puerto Rico, air media in particular, relies on the Federal Clean Air Act of 1990 and local environmental legislation has relied on the command-and-control approach to environmental policy. Seguinot-Barbosa (2011), Rodríguez-Cintrón (2002) and the regional EPA office describe the regulatory framework in the context of Puerto Rico. In particular, in Puerto Rico efforts to promote environmental conservation (e.g., preservation of green areas, protection of endangered species) and water and air quality standards rely on legislation (both federal and local) which are in essence command-and-control in nature.[2] Even though this approach has its merits, a market-based approach to environmental policy may be suitable to Puerto Rico, particularly given the arguably high rates of non-compliance (*Puerto Rico 2025*). The many benefits of putting a price on carbon emissions have not been enjoyed by the Puerto Rican economy and the debate about market-based policies has been, at best, very limited.

However, there are examples of efforts by policymakers to implement market-based policies, but these efforts arise from the imposition of federal law, particularly the Clean Air Act of 1990 (CEA). The main component of the CEA as it relates to the present work, is that it allows for the adoption of market-based incentives to meet policy goals; in particular section 110(a) (2)(A) of the CEA. In the context of Puerto Rico, Rodríguez-Cintrón (2002) mentions amendments to the Ley de Política Ambiental in 1993 (i.e., ley 87 and 60); these amendments simply follow the structure of the federal law and are put forward in order to comply with federal law. As a result, these laws, which are no longer valid, do not represent the initiative of Puerto Rican policymakers in the context of environmental policy.

The current piece of legislation in Puerto Rico about environmental policy is law 416 of 2004; this law follows the logic of the Clean Air Act of 1990. In the context of market-based mechanisms, law 416 relies on section 110(a)(2) (A) of the CEA, according to the document *Puerto Rico Environmental Quality Board Regulation for the Control of Atmospheric Pollution*. The implication here is that the current law allows, but does not force, the Puerto Rican government to control emissions using market-based mechanisms. Additionally, according to the Rodríguez-Cintrón (2002), in 1998 and 1999 another project was proposed (i.e., P. del S. 1067), but not implemented, which aimed at developing a cap and trade system. Additional projects (proposed but not approved), which allude to the implementation of a price mechanism include P. del S. 1052 in 1995, P. de la C. 3414 in 2007. Other projects also touch on the issue of air pollution, but mainly refer to assessment efforts and so no clear mandate to implement market-based policies in Puerto Rico is present (e.g., P. del S. 1061 in 2009, R.C. del S. 0170 in 2009, R.C. del S. 0350 in 2010). Additionally, Walker (1995, 48), a report commissioned in 1995 by the government of Puerto Rico, indicates that some of the key recommendations to address environmental issues in Puerto Rico (air media in particular) include installing additional, more efficient particulate matter control devices and burning fuel with lower sulfur content (this includes the power companies); these recommendations do not indicate a clear role for market-based policies.

Hence, based on the literature review and data gathered, one may conclude that there is little evidence to support the claim that sufficient efforts have been made by Puerto Rican policymakers to address environmental issues via market-based policies.

Furthermore, the *Puerto Rico 2025* project mentions, as a medium-term initiative, the implementation of market-based mechanisms, particularly in the context of business and household energy usage. In their analysis, the project conducted interviews and focus-group-type exercises with policy-makers, industry experts, among others, which resulted in policy recommendations or strategies and the degree of feasibility and priority for each strategy. In the context of market-based environmental policies, the results indicate that feasibility levels (i.e., the extent to which participants perceive that the strategy was doable or not) were not particularly high and, more importantly, the priority of such policies was not high. It is noteworthy that the reason as to why these market-based policies did not exhibit much weight is not clear, but the results from the analysis indicate that such policies are not likely to be implemented soon. I conjecture that lack of information about the benefits of such policies may partially explain the results, but more rigorous analysis is certainly needed to identify the driving factors.

Irizarry-Mora (2012) talks about some of the policy recommendations put forward by governmental, community and non-for-profits organizations. For instance, the Frente Unido Ambientalista as part of its recommendations (see "Estrategia sobre política pública energética para Puerto Rico," Frente Unido Ambiental de Puerto Rico, 27 de febrero 1994, Guayanilla, PR, mimeo) suggests that polluting firms should compensate those affected. Even though this is not a market-based policy *per se*, it highlights the need to make sure that polluting firms should be made partially responsible for the costs to society they generate through pollution activities. A different non-for-profit Puerto Rican organization, Asociación Puertorriqueña Energía Verde, proposes the use of carbon credits and the implementation of a cap and trade system; however, no further details about a cap and trade system are provided.

Additionally, Rodríguez-Inoa (2011) interviewed a non-random sample of nine experts in planning and environmental issues; fifteen open questions were provided to the interviewees in a questionnaire. Two questions from the questionnaire are relevant to the present analysis, namely, question 1 and question 4. Question 1 asked interviewees to indicate what have been some of the environmental problems affecting Puerto Rico in the past 30 years. Interestingly, one of the respondents stated that no price has been put to the services ecosystems provide; consumers and businesses utilize the ecosystem without taking into account its price. Additionally, question 4 asked respondents to talk about the solutions to environmental issues in Puerto Rico. Some of the respondents presented specific policy recommendations at the micro level such as the imposition of environmentally friendly packaging standards to local manufactures, tariffs to less environmentally friendly products, and the financing of recycling programs through municipal taxes. Even though the analysis does not talk about specific macro-level market-based policies, it indicates the importance of putting a price to the services ecosystems provide and the use of taxes to alter business and consumer behavior. Additional, in-depth analysis about policy schemes to address environmental issues are certainly needed.

This section concludes by touching on the role of community-based efforts to environmental issues in Puerto Rico, an important approach to addressing environmental issues in that country. There is evidence to suggest that since the 1960s the number of community-based organizations and degree of involvement of these organizations has increased (Zayas-Oliveras 2006). Navarro (2006), in *Guía Ambiental para Puerto Rico*, and Zayas-Oliveras (2006) in her thesis present a partial list of community-based organizations in Puerto Rico. Among the community-based organizations, Casa Pueblo is one important example.[3] Its inception in the early 1980s illustrates efforts to protect important ecological areas in Puerto Rico via community participation (for a list of its achievements see Massol et al. 2006), and demonstrates the ability of Puerto Ricans to increase community awareness and expand the size of protected areas through new legislation. The focus has been on the protection of ecological systems/areas in Puerto Rico, but no evidence was found about the use of market-based mechanisms to address environmental issues. In Massol et al. (2006) and during an informative tour taken at Casa Pueblo in the summer of 2015, mention was made about the importance of accounting for the benefits of the environment to the community and businesses (positive externalities) via a better quality of life and increase in incomes in the region with eco-tourism, but no mention was made about the potential role of emission taxes or marketable permit systems. In this context the use of this type of market-based mechanisms may help aid Casa Pueblo's efforts to address air pollution issues (perhaps a new dimension in its environmental movement) and at the same time raise revenue to finance future efforts.

In the context of air pollution, Comunidades Unidas Contra la Contaminación, CUCCO, a community-based environmental group, has fought against air pollution in the Cataño area. According to Zayas-Oliveras (2006), CUCCO has been fighting against air pollution from the Caribbean Gulf Refinery and the Puerto Rico Power Authority (see appendix P for a profile and background on CUCCO). Additionally, in her survey Zayas-Oliveras presents evidence which indicates that there is room to improve efforts to address air pollution issues in Puerto Rico. For instance, the response to question 10 of the questionnaire indicates that 12 percent of the focus of environmental issues is on air pollution, whereas water pollution and conservation are at the top of the list. This line of research shows the need to delve into air pollution issues in Puerto Rico and the lack of market-based policies related to air media.

To summarize, the literature review presented in this section indicates that additional efforts are needed to implement market-based policies in Puerto Rico, particularly given the arguably high rates of non-compliance in Puerto

Rico. An attempt to implement a cap and trade system was not completed (i.e., cap and trade system was never implemented), but it may suggest the willingness of policymakers to move forward along these lines. The literature review also suggests that there is a need to further analyze the potential role of market-based mechanisms, particularly an emission/carbon tax, in the context of Puerto Rico. Such analysis does not currently exist and could shed light into the environmental and economic benefits of an emission tax for Puerto Rico. The increasing role of communities in environmental issues may provide the support needed to implement market-based policies, particularly once the benefits are underscored. The main approach of community-based involvement seems to be the protection of important environmental areas in Puerto Rico. However, there is little evidence to support the claim that market-based policies, such as emission taxes, have been or are part of the environmental policy agenda. As a result, a more detailed study of the potential role of market-based policies in Puerto Rico is warranted.

RENEWABLE ENERGY: ROOM FOR GROWTH AND SOME POLICY EFFORTS

Efforts to employ renewable energy sources have been mixed, but Puerto Rico aims at getting 20 percent of energy from renewables by 2035 (EIA, Profile Analysis, Puerto Rico; Avilés 2011).[4] Currently, fossil fuels are the primary source of energy and so there is growing economic and environmental concerns about the reliance on these (Ladner-García and O'Neill-Carrillo 2010, 42). As of 2013 the main source of electricity came from petroleum (55%) followed by natural gas (28%) and coal (16%).[5] Solar energy water heaters have been implemented (Puerto Rico ranks fifth among US states according to the EIA) and, more recently, non-profit centers have been established to promote the use, development and implementation of new technology along with renewable energy. Examples of these centers include PREC, INTENCO, INESI and ITEAS. These centers are associated with local universities and more than likely are a result of funding (e.g., tax incentives and grants) by federal and local entities. Incentive programs in Puerto Rico to promote renewable energy include personal tax deductions and rebate programs (see DSIRE website http://programs.dsireusa.org/system/program?state=TER); the net effect of these incentives remains to be seen.

The share of renewable energy used to produce electricity in Puerto Rico in 2011 was about 1 percent. However, new energy development projects have taken place thereby raising the use of renewables from 1.15 percent of energy generation in fiscal year 2013 to 1.84 percent in fiscal year 2015.[6] Figure C.9 shows the upward trend in the generation of energy using renewables relative to total energy generated, albeit with small shares at around the 2 percent mark in mid-2015. It is noteworthy that the share of hydropower shows a downward trend (among others because of issues of maintenance) as a share of total energy generated (see figure C.10) thus suggesting a larger role of solar and wind.[7] According to a PREPA report[8] (see figure C.11), oil shows a downward trend from fiscal year 2013 to 2015, while natural gas, coal and renewables compensate this reduction in oil for the same period with natural gas playing a key role. As mentioned earlier, oil still plays a dominant role in the generation of energy as illustrated in figure C.12 by the strong positive correlation between the price per kwh and the average cost per barrel of oil.

There are two wind facilities in operation since 2012 with 120 megawatts capacity and at least two solar PV plants are in operation (EIA, Profile Analysis, Puerto Rico). These figures suggest that there is room to exploit these resources along with ocean wave energy sources as suggested by a series of papers published by ITEAS, University of Puerto Rico-Mayagüez campus, in 2009.[9] Additionally, there are an important number of utility-scale projects which promote the use of renewable energy (e.g., PV plants in Guayama, Loiza, and wind farms in Naguabo and Santa Isabel).[10] These efforts, however, seem to be segmented and thus a more unified approach may be needed to achieve potential economies of scale and an increase in the use of renewable energy.[11]

The government-based power company (PREPA) is the main generator of electricity and thus a potential market to address pollution issues in Puerto Rico (figure C.13 shows pollution levels from the consumption of energy in Puerto Rico).[12] Therefore, policy efforts must take into account this source of pollution if substantial reductions in air pollution levels are to be achieved and further use of renewables promoted.

Figure C.13 shows a relatively stable level of CO_2 emissions from energy consumption between 1980 to about 2000. Pollution then increased from to 2000 to 2006, with a drastic and clear decrease since. The reduction in emissions can be attributed to two key factors: (i) a sustained decrease in overall economic activity (e.g., reduction in the number of industrial clients) and (ii) an increase in the use of natural gas, which is a less-pollution-intensive fossil fuel. Even when the decrease in emissions is associated to a reduction in economic activity, electricity generation depends heavily on oil fuels and thus emissions can be expected to rise as the economy recovers. It is thus important to establish policy to tackle this point source of pollution.

The use of renewables to tackle pollution while satisfying energy needs has been suggested in Irizarry-Rivera, Colucci-Ríos and O'Neill-Carrillo (2010), where a comprehensive study of potential renewable energy sources for Puerto Rico is presented. In particular, the authors recommend the use of solar PV on rooftops, offshore wind farms and ocean waves as cost-effective renewable energy sources capable of satisfying the entire demand for energy. The following summarizes the results in Irizarry-Rivera, Colucci-Ríos and O'Neill-Carrillo (2010, 26): "In Puerto Rico, with our abundant renewable resources, the question should be not how to best integrate renewable resources into the existing electric energy grid or other energy infrastructures, but how our existing infrastructures and practices should change or transition in order to allow maximum use of solar, wind, ocean and other renewable energy sources." Additionally, Ladner-García and O'Neill-Carrillo (2010) show that rooftop solar PV energy may support the entire residential energy demand, but only a portion for commercial and industrial energy demand; important reductions in greenhouse gases could be achieved as a result. It is noteworthy that the available rooftop space is large enough, particularly to satisfy residential energy demand, and so aspects of land use to develop large-scale PV solar projects do not seem necessary at this point.

There have been policy efforts to encourage the use of renewable energy sources, for example, metering law, local industrial incentives, open-access law and tax credits for renewables (Ladner-García and O'Neill-Carrillo 2010, 43). The aforementioned analyses, plus the implementation of these policy efforts, could be potentially coupled with market-based mechanisms. This would encourage research and development, raise revenue to fund renewable energy projects, reduce pollution in a cost-efficient fashion and help transition the economy toward renewables by increasing the relative price of non-renewables. There are indeed country experiences on carbon-pricing schemes which could be used as a guide to implement market-based mechanisms; in general the experience has been positive (see e.g., Teitenberg 2013). Moreover, the development of a regional and perhaps an international model of a carbon-pricing scheme could also be part of the overall policy approach. This is because at the regional/international level there are potential efficiency gains to be achieved and issues of, for example, carbon leakage addressed. It remains to be seen whether current federal regulation allows policymakers in Puerto Rico the latitude necessary to undertake such a project across countries, for example, Caribbean neighbors such as the Dominican Republic and Lesser Antilles.

The mild increase in the use of renewables is not strongly correlated with the price per kwh and/or the average cost of oil (see figure C.14). Even though this increase in renewables might be due to targeted policies and to a lesser extent to higher price per kwh, figure C.14 suggests that there might be room to use a price mechanism to encourage the use of renewables and at the same time tackle air pollution. Additionally, price per kwh (as well as average cost of oil) is not strongly correlated with the level of efficiencies in the system to distribute energy thus suggesting a potential role for a price mechanism to achieve efficiency gains. For example, a tax on emissions may provide the incentives to (i) improve efficiencies in order to lower tax payments associated with pollution levels and (ii) switch to renewables by making the price of carbon relatively higher. Indeed, the literature on carbon taxes presents strong evidence of the net positive effects it has on the economy. For instance, in a series of papers as part of an edited volume by Parry, Morries and Williams (2015), the authors argue for the potential role of a carbon tax in the United States: it is shown, *inter alia*, the extent to which a carbon tax (i) can be pro-growth and help tackle budget deficit issues, (ii) may result in lower taxes across the economy (e.g., payroll taxes, corporate taxes), (iii) reduces the costs associated to pollution such as health risks and (iv) may create momentum for the implementation of similar policies at the international level.

Figure C.15 shows the non-linear inverse relationship between peak-load demand and the price per kwh. This suggests that a price mechanism (e.g., emission tax) may help reduce peak-load demand; and the revenue from this tax could be used to move energy consumption into renewables and away from oil, coal and natural gas.

Regression analysis (for a discussion on methods and data see the following section) indicates that higher oil prices are associated with lower levels of energy demand. The reason is twofold: on the one hand, a higher oil price results in higher energy prices and thus lower demand as consumers face higher prices; and on the other, higher oil prices increase production costs thereby lowering economic activity and thus the demand for energy. Even when controlling for the effects of higher oil prices on economic activity, and assuming away general equilibrium effects and fuel substitution effects, estimates indicate that an increase of 10 basis points in the rate of change of the average (trend) price of oil (as measured by the West Texas Index) reduces, *ceteris paribus*, the rate of change of total demand for energy (trend) by .12 basis points. Alternative measures for the price of oil (i.e., US price of imported crude oil and US no. 6 residual fuel oil price) yield similar results. A tax based on CO_2 content could achieve both a reduction on oil use and at the same time move consumers to renewables and, in the medium term, to natural gas.

Figure C.16 gives a sense of the extent to which PREPA's total revenue could rise as a result of higher energy prices, particularly energy prices associated to oil prices (as mentioned earlier oil still plays a dominant role in energy generation). Additional revenues could be used to promote renewable energy projects. Regression analysis indicates that, assuming away fuel substitution effects and technology improvements, an increase in the rate of change in the average (trend) price of oil by 10 basis point results in a 3.5 basis point increase in total (trend) revenue. This is consistent with a price-inelastic demand for energy.

The analysis of substitutability across fuels (i.e., renewables, coal, natural gas and oil) presents several estimation challenges, particularly in the presence of targeted policies (e.g., subsidies, tax credits). For instance, even as the price of natural gas and oil show a recent downward trend due to increases in world production, the price of solar panels keeps falling due to increases in supply at a global scale. In the case where the price of oil and natural gas exhibits a downward trend, plus the historic reliance on fossil fuels, one would expect a decrease in the use of renewables. However, because of aggressive policies, among other factors, an increase in the production of PVs and jobs created in the solar industry in the United States associated with the use of solar energy (mainly from installation), suggests that even at low prices of fossil fuels there is growth in the demand for solar energy. Figure C.17 illustrates the downward trend in the average price of PV equipment, and the *National Solar Job Census 2014* shows the rising trends in the employment associated to the solar industry in the United States, for example, although small in absolute value, solar employment increased by about 85 percent between September 2010 and November 2014.[13] These data point to the potential for growth in the solar industry in Puerto Rico. The solar industry in Puerto Rico could potentially benefit even further if it had unprotected access (currently the United States protects the solar panel industry via steep trade tariffs) to solar panels and technology from around the globe. This is particularly relevant given the key role US federal policy has played in promoting the solar industry via The Advanced Energy Manufacturing Tax Credit Program, plus uncertainties as to whether this policy will continue over a sustained period of time.[14]

Cross-country estimates of elasticities indicate the presence of short- and long-run effects in the consumption of renewables. First, there is some evidence of substitution between renewables and oil prices, and the use of renewables and income levels (e.g., Sardorsky 2009; Apergis and Payne 2014). If higher income levels are associated with the use of renewables, then Puerto Rico would be required to provide extra resources to develop renewables; one way to afford the use of renewables is via carbon-pricing policies. Moreover, if the link between the price of oil and the use of renewables is present (based on cross-country analysis), then policies to promote renewables (coupled with carbon-pricing schemes) are key to pave the way for the use of renewables. In this context, comprehensive development policy in Puerto Rico could be more aggressive.

DISCUSSION OF REGRESSION ANALYSIS

This section discusses the data and methods used in the regression results presented in the preceding section.

Monthly data ranging from August 1999 to August 2015 come from two different sources. First, monthly energy generation, consumption, sales and total revenue are from PREPA's (Puerto Rico's utility company) monthly reports (interim, unaudited) which are available in pdf format on their website.[15] Monthly data on fuel prices, index of economic activity are collected from various sources by the Puerto Rico Planning Board and available on their website in Excel format.[16]

Data on oil prices are measured in US dollars per barrel according to the West Texas Index (WTI), and the US price of imported crude oil in US dollars per barrel and US no. 6 oil residual fuel oil in cents per barrel. These data are collected and put together by the Puerto Rico Planning Board from the International Energy Agency's monthly reports. The coincident index of economic activity of Puerto Rico is maintained by the Puerto Rico Government Development Bank (GDB) with 1980 as base year. Data on total sales from PREPA is nothing but energy consumption (demand) measured in kwh in thousands (including unbilled adjustment); and total revenue data are from PREPA and measured in thousands of US dollars including unbilled adjustments. Generation of electricity from renewables also comes from PREPA. Yearly and monthly dummy variables were constructed to control for seasonal and year-specific effects. Since the main provider of energy is PREPA, data on sales and revenue come exclusively from this provider. PREPA generates about 65 percent of the electricity and the rest comes from EcoEléctrica (liquid natural gas), AES-Puerto Rico (coal) and renewable energy projects.

As for the method of analysis, a difference-in-difference estimation was employed via OLS. Data were transformed into logarithms. In order to capture medium to long-term effects (and thus correct) for short-term volatility, data were "smoothed" using the Hodrick-Prescott filter provided by the statistical software E-Views.

The following benchmark model was estimated

$$S_t = \alpha + \beta_1 WTI_t + \beta_2 IEA_t + \sum \gamma_i Z_i + \epsilon_t \tag{8.1}$$

where S_t denotes first-differenced demand for electricity, WTI_t first-differenced West Texas Index of the price of barrel of oil, α regression constant, IEA_t the monthly coincident index of economic activity in Puerto Rico by the GDB at time t, and the vector Z a set of controls including year and month dummies. Dickey-Fuller tests indicate that each series is an I(2) process. The model specification in (8.1) has several elements consistent with the model used by PREPA to prepare its forecasts of electricity demand.

The model specification seeks to estimate β_1 since such an estimate provides a sense of the sensitivity of demand with respect to the price of oil (main fuel component in energy production in Puerto Rico). In order to correct for issues of endogeneity (between sales and price of electricity) the price of oil was used as an instrument; indeed, the price of kwh is positively and highly correlated with the various measures of price of oil utilized (see figure C.18). Moreover, since the price of oil could be picking up aspects of economic activity, which in turn may reflect on the demand for electricity, the index of economic activity was used to correct this. It should be noted that residuals were modeled as an ARMA process according to the correlogram of estimated residuals. The reader is reminded that all variables were smoothed using the Hodrick-Prescott filter. Correlation coefficients indicate small correlation between WTI_t and IEA_t and so issues of multicollinearity are ruled out (see Figure C.19).

The model makes several important assumptions and presents a number of limitations, which are important to keep in mind when making policy recommendations. First, the estimation assumes that changes in technology remain constant or are small. Even though Equation (8.1) does not explicitly control for technology, it is assumed that potential effects via technology take place via changes in the price of oil, economic activity and the trend derived from the Hodrick-Prescott filter. Second, fuel substitution effects by businesses and consumers are assumed to be small. In the case of Puerto Rico this is not a strong assumption since consistently and overwhelmingly oil has been the main fuel to produce electricity (during periods of low- and high oil prices), with a relatively smaller role for natural gas since the early 2000s, and the role of renewables still very small with very little substitution toward renewables taking place. Third, the model in (8.1) does not capture dynamic macroeconomic effects as in computable general equilibrium models. These assumptions and limitations are indeed potential extensions of the model and future lines of research.

Several factors affect the demand for electricity. First, technological improvement in fossil fuel production is likely to lower the price of oil thus increasing demand for electricity; this is captured by the price of oil variable. Second, within-year weather variations, changes in regulation (e.g., EPA mandates for cleaner air), among others, are captured by month and year dummies variables, and the smoothing of the data using the Hodrick-Prescott filter. Third, income levels, population changes and the general effects of the domestic and US economic activity in the domestic economy are captured by the coincident index of economic activity. Indeed, US macroeconomic activity has historically been highly correlated with Puerto Rico's macroeconomy. Fourth, abrupt changes due to large economic shocks are corrected using dummy variables and the Hodrick-Prescott filter. Figure C.20 shows a sample of the regression estimations. Results were discussed in the preceding section.

POLICY OPTIONS AND FUTURE LINES OF RESEARCH

In order to study the applicability and effects of potential market-based policies in Puerto Rico, estimates for social damages to the environment are needed; marginal damages provide the theoretical basis to set carbon-pricing policies, for example, carbon tax. O'Neill-Carrillo et al. (2012), tables III and IV, show initial estimates for social costs in Puerto Rico by fuel type (i.e., coal, petroleum and natural gas). These may provide the basis for an initial analysis of a carbon tax, as in Metcalf (2009). Damages from air pollution are well documented in the literature and therefore back-of-the-envelope estimates could be used to measure marginal damages in the case of Puerto Rico, for example, see Lu et al. (2015) for recent estimates in the context of the United States. Further estimates of social costs in the context of Puerto Rico, however, are needed if more informed policy recommendations are to be put forward.

In terms of methodology as it relates to the one employed in this chapter, robustness checks as it pertains to each of the variables may help corroborate results. For instance, apart from the GDB index of economic activity the Puerto Rico Planning Board also publishes its own coincident index of economic activity, and PREPA publishes peak-demand loads; these alternative measures could be used to estimate the model in Equation (8.1). Furthermore, the analysis relies heavily on the use of the Hodrick-Presscott filter to account for medium- and long-term effects (e.g., technology and consumer and business behavior) and smooth the data more generally. There are a number of techniques which decompose time series data into its trend and cyclical components and so these could be used to delve into the results in future research.

Simulations on the initial and subsequent effects on the economy are also important components for policymaking which need further analysis. In this context, general equilibrium models and GIS planning tools (e.g., Xplorah in the case of Puerto Rico) may be used for this line of research. Indeed, the brief regression analysis presented in this chapter is a partial-equilibrium one, which assumes away the broader macroeconomic impacts of policy. The theoretical pillars of carbon-pricing schemes as well as country experiences with these types of policies (see Teitenberg 2013 for examples) may serve well in this line of policy inquiry.

Policy coordination is also an important line of research, particularly in the presence of existing taxes/subsidies and additional market failures in the local economy. Additionally, there are aspects of carbon leakage which are important to account for in a regional/international context. In this context, estimates using open-economy general equilibrium models will be useful in designing policy. And country-specific in-depth analysis of the price elasticity between renewables and fossil fuels is certainly needed.

An important policy option for Puerto Rico, in terms of environmental policy, is the implementation of policy in a regional setting. In particular, there are potential gains from expanding the energy market (both to buy energy from and sell to) nearby markets such as the Dominican Republic. In a carbon-pricing policy regime context, moreover, the expansion of markets to a regional setting offers important efficiency gains, including offsetting potential carbon leakages effects, as well as the development of much-needed energy infrastructure. To achieve this policymakers in Puerto Rico would need to see whether the net benefits of such policy regime could be maximized under current US regulatory framework. This is because a carbon-pricing scheme in the Caribbean may require Puerto Rico to enjoy the policy-setting autonomy to coordinate policy, that is, national sovereignty to set adequate environmental policy across countries so as to achieve market efficiency gains. The debate on environmental policy in Puerto Rico should therefore evolve around regional (and potentially an international) perspective.

NOTES

1. This chapter was written before the newly created energy board and thus its role is excluded from the analysis.

2. Recent conservation efforts by the Puerto Rican government include Executive Order OE-2008-68, Reserva Natural Ciénaga Las Cucharillas, and Executive Order OE-2008-22, Reserva Natural del Corredor Ecológico del Noreste. A recent command-and-control policy effort to address light pollution is Ley Núm. 218 of 2008.

3. Examples of non-for-profit organizations also include Estuario de la Bahía de San Juan and Comunidades del Caño Martín Peña.

4. There are a number of Executive Orders which illustrate attempts by the Puerto Rican government to stimulate the use of renewable energy sources and promote energy conservation, for example, OE-2007-41, OE-2008-32, OE-2008-33, OE-2008-34, OE-2008-35, OE-2008-36, OE-2008-47. Additionally, there are a set of laws in Puerto Rico to promote the use of renewables, for example, Ley Núm. 172 of 2007 to promote the use of solar energy via fiscal incentives; Ley Núm. 114 of 2007 and Ley Núm. 211 of 2008 to implement a net metering system; Ley Núm. 325 of 2004, Ley para el Desarrollo de Energía Renovable; Ley Núm. 145 of 2006 to promote the use renewables in the municipios of Puerto Rico.

5. See EIA website http://www.eia.gov/state/?sid=RQ

6. See http://aeepr.com/Docs/Ley57/Ley%2057%20Fuentes%20de%20Generacin%20(Portal).pdf

7. I am grateful to Dr. Efrain O'Neill for pointing out the role of maintenance in the hydropower system.

8. See http://aeepr.com/Docs/Ley57/Ley%2057%20Fuentes%20de%20Generación%20(Portal).pdf

9. See http://iteas.uprm.edu/docs/antologia ITEAS 2009.pdf

10. See EIA, Profile Analysis, Puerto Rico.

11. Capacity constraints of the current energy grid is a key limitation to integrate renewable energy source, that is, feed energy to the current system from renewable energy sources. I thank Dr. Efrain O'Neill for this comment.

12. Source: US Energy Information Agency. https://www.eia.gov/state/data.cfm?s id=RQ#CarbonDioxideEmissions. Notes on data: "...consumption of energy include emissions due to the consumption of petroleum, natural gas, and coal, and also from natural gas flaring. Carbon dioxide emissions are calculated for each individual fuel, with some refinements that are detailed below, by applying carbon emission coefficients—or million metric tons of carbon dioxide emitted per quadrillion Btu of fuel consumed—to international consumption and flaring data." For more information on data please visit https://www.eia.gov/cfapps/ipdbproject/docs/IPMNotes.html#ind

13. National Solar Job Census 2014, available http://www.thesolarfoundation.org/wp-content/uploads/2015/01/TSF-National-Census-2014-Report web.pdf

14. Department of Energy, fact sheet: 48C Manufacturing Tax Credits, http://energy.gov/downloads/fact- sheet-48c-manufacturing-tax-credits

15. See http://www.aeepr.com/INVESTORS/FinancialInformation.aspx

16. See http://www.jp.gobierno.pr/Portal JP/Default.aspx?tabid=185

Appendix A

This appendix derives Equations (4.12) and (4.13). Differentiation of (4.10) with respect to s^h and s^f yields, respectively, (subscripts denote partial derivatives)

$$W_{s^h} = (\beta q^h + t^h - s^h)nq_{s^h}^h + (\beta q^f + t^f - s^f)mq_{s^h}^f = 0 \tag{A.1}$$

$$W_{s^f} = (\beta q^f + t^f - s^f)mq_{s^f}^f + (\beta q^h + t^h - s^h)nq_{s^f}^h = 0 \tag{A.2}$$

Then, using the fact that

$$mq_{s^h}^f = nq_{s^f}^h \tag{A.3}$$

and combining (A.1) and (A.2) gives

$$\beta q^h + t^h - s^h = (\beta q^f + t^f - s^f)\left(\frac{mq_{s^f}^f}{nq_{s^h}^h}\right)^{1/2} \tag{A.4}$$

Then, substituting (A.4) back into (A.2) yields

$$\beta q^f + t^f - s^f = 0 \tag{A.5}$$

And substituting (A.5) into (A.1) gives

$$\beta q^h + t^h - s^h = 0 \tag{A.6}$$

Appendix B

The derivation of some of the expressions in the analysis is presented in this appendix.

First, obtain Cournot-Nash levels of output. Maximization of (6.3) and (6.4) yield two first-order conditions which yield the symmetric Cournot-Nash levels of output for the foreign firms, $\bar{q}^f$, and home firms, $\bar{q}^h$:

$$\omega \bar{q}^h = \beta(m+1)(\alpha - c^h) - m\gamma(\alpha - c^f) \tag{B.1}$$

$$\omega \bar{q}^f = \beta(n+1)(\alpha - c^f) - n\gamma(\alpha - c^h) \tag{B.2}$$

where

$$\omega = \beta^2(n+1)(m+1) - nm\gamma^2 > 0 \tag{B.3}$$

Additionally,

$$p^h = \alpha - n\beta\bar{q}^h - m\gamma\bar{q}^f \Rightarrow \omega \ p_\delta^h = \beta m(k^h - k^f) \tag{B.4}$$

Obtain the expression of

$$\bar{\delta}. \tag{B.5}$$

Differentiation of the welfare function (6.12) gives

$$\frac{\partial W^h}{\partial \delta} = mq^f \left(k^h - \frac{\partial p^f}{\partial \delta} \right) + np^h \frac{\partial q^h}{\partial \delta} + m\delta k^h \frac{\partial q^f}{\partial \delta} = 0 \tag{B.6}$$

where

$$p_\delta^f = \frac{(k^h - k^f)m(\beta^2(n+1) - n\gamma^2)}{\omega}; \ \omega \bar{q}_\delta^h = m\gamma(k^h - k^f); \ \omega \bar{q}_\delta^f = -\beta(n+1)(k^h - k^f) \tag{B.7}$$

Substitution of these into the welfare-maximizing first-order condition and simplification gives $\bar{\delta}$:

$$\Omega\bar{\delta} = nq_\delta^h\left[\alpha\beta(\beta(m+1) - \gamma m) + \beta\gamma mk^f + nk^h(\beta^2(m+1) - m\gamma^2)\right] - \\ (p_\delta^f - k^h)(\alpha - k^f)(\beta(n+1) - n\gamma) > 0 \tag{B.8}$$

where

$$0 < \Omega = (k^h - k^f)\beta m\left[k^h(\beta^2(n+1)^2(m+2) - (n+2)mn\gamma^2) + mk^f(\beta^2(n+1)^2 - n^2\gamma^2)\right] \tag{B.9}$$

and

$$0 > p_\delta^f - k^h = (-\beta^2(n+1)k^h - mk^f(\beta^2(n+1) - n\gamma^2))/\omega, \tag{B.10}$$

$$q_\delta^h > 0, \beta(n+1)(\alpha - k^f) - n\gamma(\alpha - k^f) > 0 \tag{B.11}$$

Derivation of Equation (6.15). Total differentiation of

$$W_\delta^h(\bar{\delta}(n), n) = 0 \tag{B.12}$$

yields

$$-W_{\delta\delta}^h\bar{\delta}_n = \left(p^h q_\delta^h + np^h q_{\delta n}^h + nq_\delta^h p_n^h\right) + mq_n^f(k^h - p_\delta^f) - mq^f p_{\delta n}^f - \delta m\, k^h\, q_\delta^f \tag{B.13}$$

where

$$W_{\delta\delta}^h < 0. \tag{B.14}$$

Also,

$$p_{\delta n}^f = -(k^h - k^f)\beta^h\beta^f\gamma^2/\omega^2; \quad q_{\delta n}^h = -\gamma m(k^h - k^f)(\beta^h\beta^f(n+1) - m\gamma^2)/\omega^2 \tag{B.15}$$

$$q_n^f = -\frac{\beta^h\gamma q^h}{\omega} > 0; \quad p_n^f = -\gamma q^h(\beta^h\beta^f(m+1) - m\gamma^2)/\omega \quad < 0 \tag{B.16}$$

$$p_n^h = -\beta^h q^h(\beta^h\beta^f(m+1) - m\gamma^2)/\omega \ < 0; \quad p_n^h = \frac{q^h\beta^h\beta^f(m+1)}{\omega} > 0 \tag{B.17}$$

Substitution of these into (B.13) yields Equation (6.15).

Appendix C

FIGURES

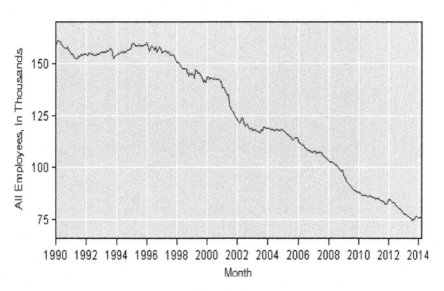

Figure C.1 Total Employment Manufacturing Sector in Puerto Rico (1990–2013), Seasonally Adjusted. Bureau of Labor Statistics.

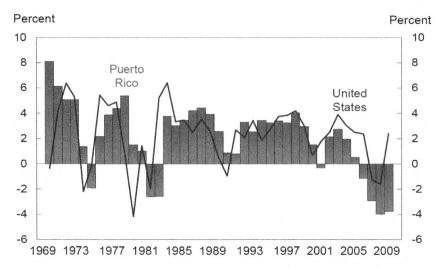

Figure C.2   Real GNP Growth. Reproduced by permission from Federal Reserve Bank of New York, "Report on the Competitiveness of Puerto Rico's Economy," June 2012.

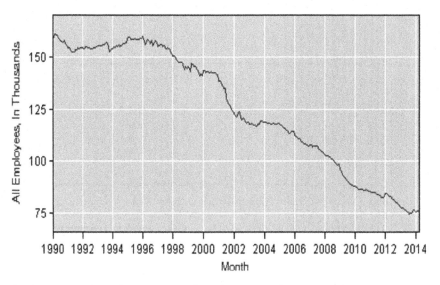

Figure C.3   Total Employment Manufacturing Sector in Puerto Rico (1990–2013), Seasonally Adjusted. Bureau of Labor Statistics.

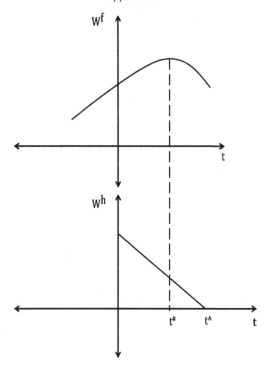

Figure C.4   Welfare and the Tax. Created by the author.

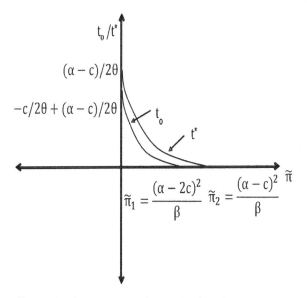

Figure C.5   Welfare Gains from Large Profits. Created by the author.

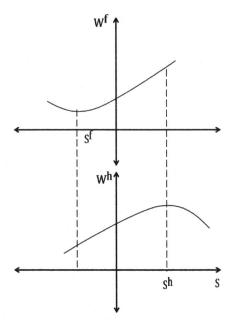

Figure C.6   Welfare and the Subsidy. Created by the author.

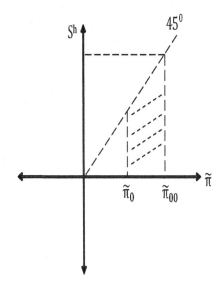

Figure C.7   Profits and the Subsidy. Created by the author.

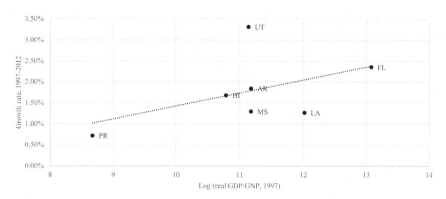

Figure C.8 Non-convergence (1997–2012): Selected US States and Puerto Rico. Created by the author from Luciano (2014).

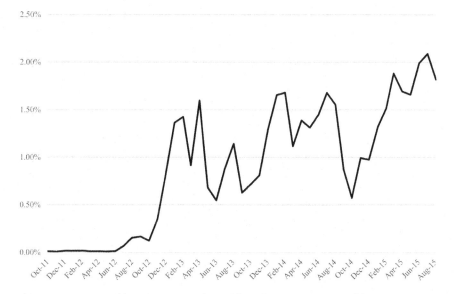

Figure C.9 Renewable Energy as a Share of Total Energy Generated in Puerto Rico: October 2011–August 2015. PREPA Monthly Report to the Governing Board.

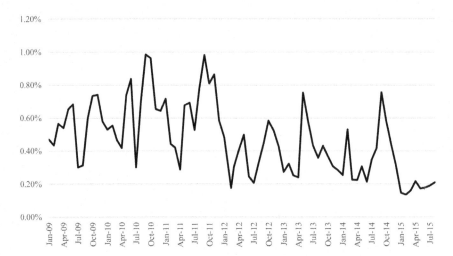

Figure C.10   Hydropower Energy as a Share of Total Energy Generated in Puerto Rico: January 2009–August 2015. PREPA Monthly Report to the Governing Board.

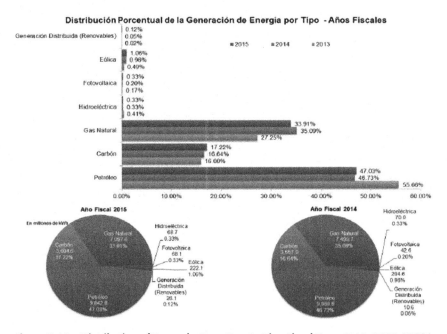

Figure C.11   Distribution of Energy by Type: Puerto Rico Fiscal Years 2013–2015. PREPA website.

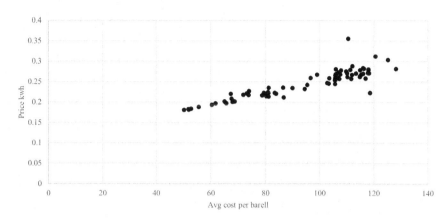

Figure C.12   Price Kwh and Average Cost per Barrel of Oil: Puerto Rico January 2009–August 2015. Data PREPA Monthly Report to the Governing Board.

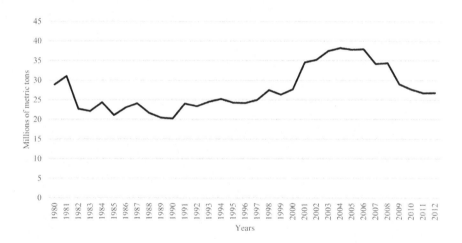

Figure C.13   Carbon dioxide emissions from consumption of energy: Puerto Rico 1980-2012. US Energy Information Agency.

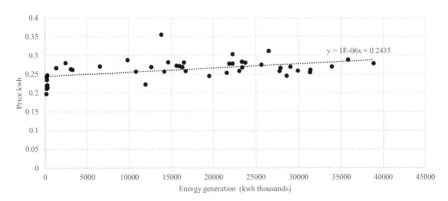

Figure C.14   Price Kwh and Generation with Renewables (Excludes Hydropower): Puerto Rico January 2011–August 2015. PREPA Monthly Report to the Governing Board.

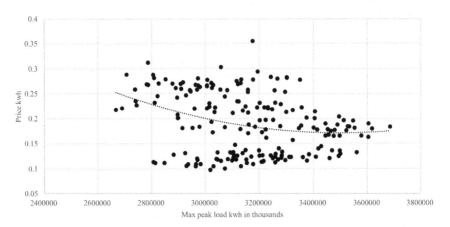

Figure C.15   Price Kwh and Maximum Peak Load Demand: Puerto Rico July 1999– August 2015. PREPA Monthly Report to the Governing Board.

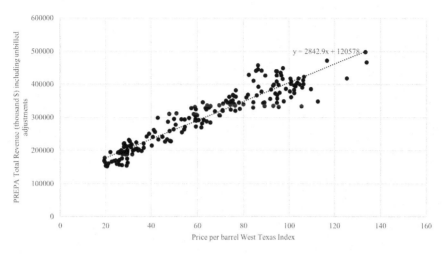

Figure C.16 WTI Price per Barrel and Total Revenue PREPA. Puerto Rico Planning Board and PREPA.

Average price of photovoltaic cells and modules, 2003-2012
dollars per peak watt

Year	Average Prices Cells	Modules
2003	1.86	3.17
2004	1.92	2.99
2005	2.17	3.19
2006	2.03	3.50
2007	2.22	3.37
2008	1.94	3.49
2009	1.27	2.79
2010	1.13	1.96
2011	0.92	1.59
2012	1.00	1.15

Note: Dollars are not adjusted for inflation.
Source: U.S. Energy Information Administration, Form EIA-63B, "Annual Photovoltaic Cell/Module Shipments Report."

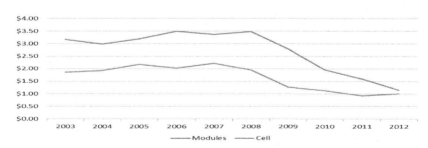

Figure C.17 Average Price of Photovoltaic Cells and Modules: 2003–2012. US Energy Information administration. "Annual Photovoltaic Cell/Module Shipments Report", Table 4 and figure 2.

Appendix C

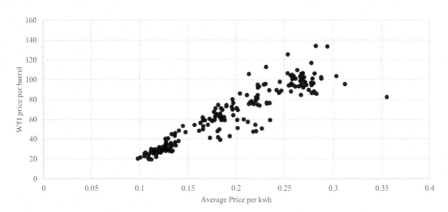

Figure C.18   Average Price of Electricity (Kwh) and price of oil per barrel (WTI). Puerto Rico Planning Board and PREPA.

	D(LOG(TRE V_TREND))	D(LOG(WTI _TREND))	D(LOG(GDBIE A_TREND))	D(LOG(SALES _T_TREND))	D(LOG(P_ TREND))
D(LOG(TREV_ TREND))	1	0.983711	0.47956	0.417917	0.977119
D(LOG(WTI_T REND))	0.983711	1	0.545137	0.446696	0.948733
D(LOG(GDBIE A_TREND))	0.47956	0.545137	1	0.887941	0.30295
D(LOG(SALES _T_TREND))	0.417917	0.446696	0.887941	1	0.217471
D(LOG(P_TRE ND))	0.977119	0.948733	0.30295	0.217471	1

Figure C.19   Correlation Coefficients Selected Variables. Created by the author.

Dependent variable: Energy Consumption - D(LOG(SALES_TREND))	(1)	(2)	(3)	(4)	(5)
Intercept	0.0004	0.0004	-.0001	5.92E-05	-.001
	(.0007)	(.0007)	(.101)	(.744)	(.003)
D(LOG(WTI_TREND))	0.0386	0.0386	0.0091	4.27E-05	-.0128
	(.0002)	(.0002)	(.532)	(.996)	(.039)
D(LOG(GDBIEA_TREND))				.8377	
				(.000)	
D(LOG(GDBIEA_TREND))_(t-13)					.3702
					(.019)
Monthly dummies	No	Yes	Yes	Yes	Yes
ARMA terms	No	No	Yes	Yes	Yes
Adj-R^2	.0675	.0723	.9999	.9999	.999
DW-stat	.0019	.0022	2.053	2.09	2.00
N	193	193	169	133	120

Dependent Variable: Total Revenue - D(LOG(TREV_TREND))	(1)	(2)	(3)	(4)	(5)
Intercept	0.0013	0.0013	.0012	.0019	.001
	(.000)	(.007)	(.353)	(.108)	(.558)
D(LOG(WTI_TREND))	0.4802	0.4802	.3575	.3850	.3742
	(.0000)	(.0000)	(.0000)	(.0000)	(.0000)
D(LOG(GDBIEA_TREND))				.3454	
				(.6039)	
D(LOG(GDBIEA_TREND))_(t-13)					-.2344
					(.7463)
Monthly dummies	No	Yes	Yes	Yes	Yes
ARMA terms	No	No	Yes	Yes	Yes
Adj-R^2	.9101	.9012	1.000	1.000	1.000
DW-stat	.005	.007	2.19	1.96	2.03
N	193	193	190	153	140

Figure C.20   Sample Regressions: Demand and Total Revenue as Dependent Variables.
P-value in Parenthesis. "December" Reference Period. ARMA Structure Vary. Created by the author.

References

Adams, L. Régibeau, and K. Rockett. "Incentives to Create Jobs: Regional Subsidies, National Trade Policy and Foreign Direct Investment." *Journal of Public Economics* 111 (2014): 102–119.

Ado, R. "Local Content Policy and the WTO Rules of Trade-Related Investment Measures (Trims): The Pros and Cons." *International Journal of Business and Management Studies* 2, no. 1 (2013): 137–146.

Albizu-Campos, P. *Comercio, riqueza y soberanía.* 1986. Reprint, San Juan, Puerto Rico: Editorial Partido Nacionalista, 1930.

———. *Obras escogidas.* Edited by J. Benjamín-Torres. Vol. I, II, III. San Juan, Puerto Rico: Editorial Jelofe, 1975.

Alvaredo, F., A. B. Atikson, T. Picketty, and E., Saez. "The Top 1 Percent in International and Historical Perspective." *Journal of Economic Perspectives* 27, no. 3 (2013): 3–20.

Apergis, N., and J. E. Payne. "Renewable Energy, Output, CO2 Emissions, and Fossil Fuel Prices in Central America: Evidence from a Nonlinear Panel Smooth Transition Vector Error Correction Mode." *Energy Economics* 42 (2014): 226–232.

Atems, B. "A Note on the Determinants of Long-Run Aggregate State Productivity Growth." *Applied Economics Letters* 22, no. 16 (2015): 1287–1292.

Atlas, C. M., T. A. Gillian, R.J. Hendershott, and M. A. Zupan. "Slicing the Federal Government Net Spending Pie: Who Wins, Who Loses, and Why." *American Economic Review* 85 (1995): 624–629.

Avilés, L. "La Cartera de Energía Renovable de Puerto Rico: ¿Demasiado Poco, Demasiado Tarde?" *University of Puerto Rico Law Review* 81 (2011): 135–172.

Baily, M. N. and B. Bosworth. "US Manufacturing Firms: Understanding its Past and its Potential Future." *Journal of Economic Perspectives* 28, no. 1 (2014): 3–26.

Barros, P. P. and L. Cabral. "Competing for Foreign Direct Investment." *Review of International Economics* 8, no. 2 (2000): 360–371.

Baumol, W. J. and E. N. Wolff. "Catching Up in the Postwar Period: Puerto Rico as the Fifth "Tigar"?" *World Development* 24, no. 5 (1996): 869–885.

Bayındır-Upmann, T. "Strategic Environmental Policy under Free Entry of Firms." *Review of International Economics* 11 (2003): 379–396.

Bellemare, M. F. and N. Carnes. "Why do Members of Congress Support Agricultural Protection?" *Food Policy* 50 (2015): 20–34.

Bénassy-Quéré, A., L. Fontagné and A. Lahrèche-Révil. "How Does FDI React To Corporate Taxation?" *International Tax and Public Finance* 12 (2005): 583–603.

Bertrand, M., M. Bombardini and F. Trebbi. *Is it whom you know or what you know? An Empirical Assessment of the Lobbying Process.* Working Paper no. 16765. NBER. 2011.

Bjorvatn, K. and C. Eckel. "Policy Competition for Foreign Direct Investment between Asymmetric Countries." *European Economic Review* 50 (2006): 1891–1907.

Blanco-Peck, R. "Política fiscal federal en Puerto Rico: modelo correlacional de consecuencias electorales." *Revista de Administración Pública* 41, no. 1 (2009): 1–22. http://journals.upr.edu/index.php/ap/article/view/301 (accessed February 7, 2017).

Bloomfield, R. J. "Introductory Chapter." In *The search for national policy.* Bloomfield, R.J. ed. Puerto Rico: Westview Press, 1985.

Bombardini, M. and F. Trebbi. "Competition and Political Organization: Together or Alone in Lobbying for Trade Policy?" *Journal of International Economics* 87, no. 1 (2012): 18–26.

Bosworth, B. P. and S. M. Collins. "*Economic growth.*" Quoted in Collins, S. M., Bosworth, B. P. and M. A. Soto-Class (eds.) *Restoring Growth in Puerto Rico: Overview and policy options.* Washington DC: Brookings Institution Press, 2006.

Bown, C. P. and M. A. Crowley. *The empirical landscape of trade policy.* Working Paper no. Policy Research 7520. World Bank. 2016.

Brander, J. A. and B. J. Spencer. "Foreign Direct Investment with Unemployment and Endogenous Taxes and Tariffs." *Journal of International Economics* 22 (1987): 257–279.

Breuer, J. B., W. Hauk and J. McDermott. "The Return of Convergence in the US States." *Applied Economic Letters* 21, no. 1 (2014): 64–68.

Bucovetsky, S. "Asymmetric Tax Competition." *Journal of Urban Economics* 30 (1991):167–181.

Carlino, G. and R. Voith. "Accounting for Differences in Aggregate State Productivity." *Regional Science and Urban Economics* 22, no. 4 (1992): 597–617.

Carro, Juan Pablo. "Deconstructing Sovereignty: The Validity of the Status-Driven Mindset as Seen through Soberanías Exitosas: Seis Modelos para el Desarrollo Económico de Puerto Rico by Angel Collado Schwarz." *Rev. Jur. UPR* 80, (2011): 439–883. http://heinonline.org/HOL/LandingPage?handle=hein.journals/rjupurco80&div=20&id=&page= (accessed February 17, 2017).

Catalá, F. "La economía de Puerto Rico: del enclave colonial al imperativo de la independencia." In *Puero Rico Nación Independiente: Imperativo del Siglo XXI.* Editora Corripio ed. Dominican Republic, 2010.

———. Promesa Rota. Una mirada institucionalista a partir de Tugwell. Ediciones Callejón ed. 2013

Chin, L., Rusli, C., and A. Khusyairi. "The Determinants of Non-Tariff Barriers: The Role of WTO Membership." *International Journal of Economics and Management* 9, no. 1 (2015): 155–176.

Choi, C-Y., and X. Wang. "Discounting of Output Convergence within the United States: Why Has the Course Changed?" *Economic Inquiry* 53, no. 1 (2015):49–71.

Clark, V. S. *Porto Rico and Its Problems*. Washington, DC: The Brookings Institution, 1930.

Collado-Schwarz, A. *Decolonization Models for America's Last Colony*. Puerto Rico: Syracuse University Press, 2012.

Collins, S.M., Bosworth, B.P. and Soto-Class, M.A. *Restoring Growth in Puerto Rico: Overview and Policy Options*. Washington DC: Brookings Institution Press, 2006.

Concepción, C. M. *Environmental policy and industrialization: The politics of regulation in Puerto Rico*. PhD diss., Berkley University.

Curet, E. *Economía política de Puerto Rico: 1950 a 2000*. San Juan, Puerto Rico: Ediciones M.A.C, 2003.

———. *Puerto Rico: Development by Integration to the US*. Editorial Cultural ed. Río Piedras, Puerto Rico, 1986.

Dean, J. M. *Do preferential trade agreements promote growth? An Evaluation of the Caribbean Basin Economic Recovery Act*. Working paper no. 2002–07-A. US International Trade Commission, Office of Economics. 2002. Accessed February 15, 2017. http://www.usitc.gov/publications/332/working papers/EC0207A.pdf.

Delpillis, L. 2013. Americas strange trade policy makes your jeans more expensive than they should be. Washington Post. October 9.

Denicol`o, V. and M. Matteuzzi. "Specific and Ad Valorem Taxation in Asymmetric Cournot Oligopolies." *International Tax and Public Finance* 7 (2000): 335–344.

Dietz, J. *Economic History of Puerto Rico: Institutional Change and Capitalist Development*. Princeton, New Jersey: Princeton University Press, 1986.

———. *Puerto Rico: Negotiating Development and Change*. Colorado: Lynne Rienner Publishers, 2003.

Dixit, A., G. M. Grossman, and E. Helpman. "Common Agency and Coordination: General Theory and Application to Government Policy Making." *Journal of Political Economy* 105, no. 4 (1997): 752–769.

Dollar, D. "Outward-Oriented Developing Economies Really Do grow more rapidly: Evidence from 95 LDCs, 1976–1985." *Economic Development and Cultural Change* 40 (1992): 523–544.

Dollar, D. and A. Kraay. "Trade, growth and poverty." *The Economic Journal* 114, no. 493 (2004): F22–F49.

Dunn, L. "The Impact of Political Dependence on Small Island Jurisdictions." *World Development* 39, no. 12 (2011): 2132–2146.

Duprey-Selgado, N. R. *A la vuelta de la esquina: el Proyecto Tydings de independencia para Puerto Rico y el diseño de una política colonial estadounidense*. Humacao, Puerto Rico: Model Offset Printing (MOP), 2016.

Dypski, M. C. "The Caribbean Basin Initiative: An Examination of Structural Dependency, Good Neighbor Relations, and American Investment." *Journal of Transnational Law and Policy* 12 (2002): 95–136.

Economic Commission for Latin America and the Caribbean (ECLAC). *The Convergent/Divergent Economic Trajectories of Puerto Rico and the United States*. Report no. LC/CAR/L.11. 2004. http://www.cepal.org/publicaciones/xml/3/14803/L0011. pdf (accessed February 13, 2017).

Egger, P., Francois, J., Manchin, M., D. Nelson. "Non-Tariff Barriers, Integration and the Transatlantic Economy." *Economic Policy* 30, no.83 (2015): 539–584.

Eller, S. F. and K. A. Wink. "The Effects of Local Economic Development Efforts: An Empirical Assessment of Expenditures on Income Growth in North Carolina Countries." *American Politics Quarterly* 26, no. 2 (1998): 196–217.

Elliot, R. J. R. and Y. Zhou. "Environmental Regulation Induced Foreign Direct Investment." *Environmental & Resource Economics* 55 (2013): 141–158.

Esteves, A. M., Coyne, B., and A. Moreno. "Local content initiatives: Enhancing the subnational benefits of the oil, gas and mining sectors." *Natural Resource Governance Institute Briefing* (2013). http://www.resourcegovernance.org/sites/default/files/Sub_Enhance_Benefits_20151125.pdf (accessed February 13, 2017).

European Commission (EC). *U.S. Barriers to Trade and Investment Report for 2008.* Report. European Commission, 2009.

Federal Reserve Bank of New York. *Report of the Competitiveness of Puerto Rico's Economy.* Report. 2012. https://www.newyorkfed.org/regional/puertorico/index. html (accessed February 13, 2017).

Finn, B. P. "Puerto Rico's economic development: The old formula no longer works: A new strategy is needed." In *Puerto Rico: The Search for National Policy.* Bloomfield, R.J. ed. Boulder, Colorado: Westview Press, 1985.

Frankel, J. and D. Romer. "Does trade cause growth?" *American Economic Review* 89 (1999): 379–399.

Fuentes-Ramírez, J. "An Approximation of Puerto Rico's Human Development Index." *Caribbean Studies* 42, no. 1 (2014): 253–258.

Fuest, C. "The Economic Integration and Tax Policy with Endogenous Foreign Ownership." *Journal of Public Economics* 89 (2005): 1823–1840.

Gamaliel-Ramos, A. *Islas migajas: Los países no independientes del Caribe contemporáneo.* Travesier & Leduc: San Juan, Puerto Rico, 2016.

Gautier, L. "Multilateral Policy Reform of Emission Taxes and Abatement Subsidies in a Two-Country Model with Oligopolistic Interdependence." *Environmental Economics and Policy Studies* 15, no. 1 (2013): 59–71.

———. "Policy Reform of Emission Taxes and Environmental Research and Development Incentives in an International Cournot Model with Product Differentiation." *Environment and Development Economics* 19, no. 4 (2014): 440–465.

———. "Emission Taxes and Product Differentiation in the Presence of Foreign Firms." *Journal of Public Economic Theory* 19, no. 2 (2017): 461–489.

———. "Local Content and Emission Taxes when the Number of Firms Is Endogenous." *Journal of Economics*, 2017b. doi: 10.1007/s00712–017–0541–9.

González, A. J. *Economía política de Puerto Rico.* San Juan, Puerto Rico: Editorial Cordillera, 1967.

González-Vazquez, E. "Environmental Financial Indicators: An economic perspective in pollution prevention opportunities in Puerto Rico." MBA thesis., University of Puerto Rico., 2001.

Government Accountability Office (GAO). *Puerto Rico: Potential Federal Income Tax Revenues Resulting from Statehood.* Report no. GGD-98–166R. GAO. General Accountability Office, 1998.

Government of Puerto Rico. *Puerto Rico 2025.* Report. DVD-ROM, A.T. Kearney. 2003.

Grossman, M. "American Public Opinion, Advocacy, and Policy in Congress: What the Public Wants and what it gets." *Public Opinion Quarterly* 79, no. 1 (2015): 204–206.

Grossman, G. M. and E. Helpman. *Special Interest Politics.* Cambridge, MA: MIT Press, 2001.

Grossman, H. I. and M. F. Iyigun. "The Profitability of Colonial Investment." *Economics and Politics* 7, no. 3 (1995): 229–241.

Haufler, A. and I. Wooton. "Country Size and Tax Competition for Foreign Direct Investment." *Journal of Public Economics* 71 (1999): 121–139.

———. "The Effects of Regional Tax and Subsidy Coordination for Foreign Direct Investment." *European Economic Review* 50, no. 2 (2006): 285–305.

Herrero-Rodríguez, J. A., A. L. Soriano-Miranda and J. V. Mari. "El efecto del régimen actual del comercio exterior, en relación al transporte marítimo, sobre la economía de Puerto Rico." *Estudio presentado ante la Comisión de Asuntos Federales e Internacionales de la Cámara de Representantes en torno a la Resolución de la Cámara 436,* del 13 de febrero de 2001.

Holmes, M. J., J. Otero and T. Panagiotidis. "A Note on the Extent of US Regional Income Convergence." *Macroeconomic Dynamics* 18, no. 7 (2014): 1635–1655.

Hoover, G. A. and P. Pecorino. "The Political Determinants of Federal Expenditure at the State Level." *Public Choice* 123 (2005): 95–113.

Hováth, Z., Moore, B. D., and J. C. Rork. "Does Federal Aid to States Aid the States." *Growth and Change* 45, no. 2 (2014): 333–361.

Irizarry-Mora, E. *Economía de Puerto Rico.* 2nd edition. Mexico: McGraw Hill Interamericana, 2011.

———. *Fuentes energéticas, luchas comunitarias y medioambiente en Puerto Rico.* Editorial de la Universidad de Puerto Rico, 2012.

Irizarry-Rivera, A. A., Colucci-Ríos, J. A. and E. O'Neill-Carrillo. "Achievable renewable energy targets for Puerto Rico's renewable energy portfolio standard." (2010) Quoted in E. O'Neill-Carrillo (ed.) *Energía Sostenible: Antología de lecturas del Instituto Tropical de Energía.* Ambiente y Sociedad (ITEAS) no. 2, 2009. http://iteas.uprm.edu/docs/antologia ITEAS 2009.pdf (accessed February 17, 2017).

Ishikawa, J. and B. J. Spencer. "Rent-Shifting Export Subsidies with Imported Intermediate Product." *Journal of International Economics* 48 (1999): 199–232.

Janeba, E. "Foreign Direct Investment under Oligopoly: Profit Shifting or Profit Capturing?" *Journal of Public Economics* 60 (1996): 423–445.

———. "Tax Competition in Imperfectly Competitive Markets." *Journal of International Economics* 44 (1998): 135–153.

———. "Tax Competition When Governments Lack Commitment: Excess Capacity as a Countervailing Threat." *American Economic Review* 90, no. 5 (2000): 1508–1519.

Jouanjean, M. A., Maur, J. C., and B. Shepherd. "US Phytosanitary Restrictions: The Forgotten Non-Tariff Barrier." *Journal of International Trade Law and Policy* 15 (2015): 2–27.

Kang, K. "Policy Influence and Private Returns from Lobbying in the Energy Sector." *Review of Economic Studies* 83, no. 1 (2015):269–305.

Kayalica, M. Ö. and S. Lahiri. "Strategic Environmental Policies in the Presence of Foreign Direct Investment." *Environmental & Resource Economics* 30 (2005):1–21.

Kayalica, M. Ö. and E. Yilmaz. "Trade and Foreign Direct Investment Linkages: FDI versus Imports." *EconoQuantum* 1 (2004): 49–63.

Keen, M. and K. A. Konrad. "The Theory of Tax Competition and Coordination." *Handbook of Public Economics* 5 (2013): 257–328.

Knight, B. "Estimating the Values of Proposal Power." *The American Economic Review* 95, no. 5 (2005): 1639–1652.

———. "Legislative Representation, Bargaining Power, and the Distribution of Federal Funds: Evidence from the US Senate." *The Economic Journal* 118, no. 532 (2008): 1785–1803.

Krugman, P. and M. Obstfeld. *International Economics: Trade and Policy.* 8th ed. Boston, MA: Prentice Hall, 2009.

Krueger, A. N., R. Teja, and A. Wolfe. *Puerto Rico-A way forward.* Report. Government Development Bank. 2015. http://www.gdb-pur.com/documents/FinalUpdatedReport7–13–15.pdf (accessed February 17, 2017).

Ladner-García, H.P. and E. O'Neill-Carrillo. "Determining realistic photovoltaic generation targets in an isolated power system." (2010) Quoted in E. O'Neill- Carrillo (ed.) *Energía Sostenible: Antología de lecturas del Instituto Tropical de Energía.* Ambiente y Sociedad (ITEAS) no. 2, 2009. http://iteas.uprm.edu/docs/antologia ITEAS 2009.pdf (accessed February 17, 2017).

Lahiri, S. and Y. Ono. "Foreign Direct Investment, Local Content Requirement, and Profit Taxation." *The Economic Journal* 108 (1998): 444–457.

———. "Export Oriented Foreign Direct Investment and Local Content Requirement." *Pacific Economic Review* 8, no. 1 (2003): 1–14.

———. *Trade and Industrial Policy under International Oligopoly.* Cambridge, UK: Cambridge University Press, 2004.

Lahiri, S. and G. Symeonidis. "Piecemeal Multilateral Environmental Policy Reforms under Asymmetric Oligopoly." *Journal of Public Economic Theory* 9 (2007): 885–899.

Lara, J. *La ruta difícil de la recuperación.* Diálogo, 19 de marzo de 2014.

———. "La perspectiva de la competitividad en el tema de la estadidad," in *Efectos sobre la competitividad de Puerto Rico de posibles cambios en la Ley 600,* (2014). http://economia.uprrp.edu/INFORMEFinalEstudioLey%20600.pdf (accessed February 17, 2017).

Lawrence, R. and A. Datla "Shaping the future of solar power: Climate change, industrial policy, and free trade Harvard Kennedy School Case, case number 1992.0, 2013.

Lawrence, R. and J. Lara. "Trade performance and industrial policy." (2006) Quoted in Collins, S. M., B. P. Bosworth, and M. A. Soto-Class (eds.) *Restoring Growth in Puerto Rico: Overview of Policy Options.* The Brookings Institution Press.

Levitt, S.D. and J.M. Poterba. "Congressional Distributive Politics and State Economic Performance." *Public Choice* 99 (1999): 185–216.

Loomis, J. and L.E. Santiago. "Recreation Benefits of Natural Area Characteristics at the El Yunque National Forest." *Journal of Environmental Planning and Management* 52, no. 4 (2009): 535–547.

———. "Testing Differences in Estimation of River Recreation Benefits for International and Domestic Tourists as a Function of Single- Versus Multiple-Destination Day Trips." *Journal of Hospitality Marketing and Management* 20 (2011): 143–165.

———. "Economic Valuation of Beach Quality Improvements: Comparing Incremental Attribute Values Estimated from Two Stated Preference Valuation Methods." *Costal Management* 41 (2013): 75–86.

Lu, X., D. W. Kicklighter, J. M. Melillo, J. M. Reilly and L. Xu. "Land Carbon Sequestration within the Conterminous United States: Regional-and State-Level Analyses." *Journal of Geophysical Research: Biogeosciences* 120, no. 2 (2015): 379–398.

Luciano, I. "El debate sobre la estadidad como vehículo de convergencia en crecimiento económico," in *Efectos sobre la competitividad de Puerto Rico de posibles cambios en la Ley 600*, (2014). http://economia.uprrp.edu/INFORMEFinalEstudioLey%20600.pdf (accessed February 17, 2017).

Massol-González, Alexis, González, Edgardo, Massol-Deyá, Arturo, and Tighe Geoghegan. vol.12 of *Bosque del Pueblo, Puerto Rico: Como la lucha antiminera cambio la política forestal desde la base comunitaria: políticas exitosas para los bosques y la gente*. London: International Institute for Environment and Development, 2006.

Marques-Velasco, R. *Un nuevo modelo económico para Puerto Rico: estrategias para el desarrollo de la industria y la agricultura local*. First Book Publishing of Puerto Rico, 1993.

Mercier, S. "Review of US farm programs." AGree-Transforming Food & Ag Policy. 2011. Accessed February 14, 2017. http:foodandagpolicy.org.

Myles, G.D. "Imperfect Competition and the Optimal Combination of *Ad Valorem* and Specific Taxation." *International Tax and Public Finance* 3 (1996): 29–44.

Mutti, J. H. *Foreign direct investment and tax competition*. Report. Institute for International Economics. 2003.

Negrón-Rivera, E. "Tax Related Industrial Inventive Impact of Political Status Options for Puerto Rico." *Boletín de Economía* Unidad de Investigaciones Económicas II, no. 4 (1997): 22–26.

Nogués, J.J., Olechowski, A., L.A. Winters. "The Extent of Nontariff Barriers to Industrial Countries' Imports." *The World Bank Economic Review* 1, no.1 (1986): 181–199.

OECD, "Foreign direct investment and the environment." OECD Proceedings, 1999.

Office of the United States Trade Representative (USTR). *2013 National trade estimate report on foreign trade barriers*. Report. Office of the United States Trade Representative. NTE, 2013.

O'Neill-Carrillo, Efrain, Zamot HR., Hernández M, Irizarry-Rivera AA., and LO Jimenez-Rodríguez. "Beyond traditional power systems: Energy externalities, ethics and society." *2012 IEEE International Symposium on Sustainable Systems and Technology (ISSST)*, 2012. doi: 10.1109/ISSST.2012.6228003

Parry, I., A. Morries, and R. C. William. *Implementing a US Carbon Tax*. London: Routledge, 2015.

Pizzini, M.V. "Una mirada al mundo de los pescadores en Puerto Rico: una perspectiva global." *Programa de Colegio Sea Grant de la Universidad de Puerto Rico*, (2011). seagrantpr.org/wp-content/uploads/2014/11/Mirada_al_mundo_de_los_pescadores.pdf (accessed February 17, 2017).

Puerto Rico Climate Change Council (PRCCC). *Climate Change and Puerto Rico's Society and Economy*. Report no. Working Group 3. Puerto Rico Climate Change Council. http://drna.gobierno.pr/oficinas/arn/recursosvivientes/costasreservasrefugios/pmzc/prccc/prccc-2013/WG3.pdf (accessed February 13, 2017).

Puerto Rico: Information on How Statehood Would Potentially Affect Selected Federal Programs and Revenue Sources. Report. GAO. General Accountability Office, 2014. 14–31.

Qiu, L.D. and Z. Tao. "Export, Foreign Direct Investment, and Local Content Requirement." *Journal of Development Economics* 66 (2001): 101–125.

Raff, H. "Preferential Trade Agreements and Tax Competition for Foreign Direct Investment." *Journal of Public Economics* 88, no. 12 (2004): 2745–2763.

Ramcharran, H. "The Pharmaceutical Industry of Puerto Rico: Ramifications of Global Competition." *Journal of Policy Modeling* 33 (2011): 395–406.

Rivera-Ortiz, A.I., I. E. Alegría-Ortega and W. Lockwood. "Las relaciones económicas de Puerto Rico en la Cuenca del Caribe: perspectivas de autonomía relativa o de subordinación." (1990). Quoted in Gautier-Mayoral, C., A.I. Rivera-Ortiz and I.E. Alegría-Ortega (eds.) *Puerto Rico en la economía política del Caribe*. Rio Piedras, Puerto Rico: Ediciones Huracán.

Rodríguez-Cintrón, E. "Los mecanismos de mercado en el control de la contaminación de aire: un enfoque adecuado para Puerto Rico?" MA thesis, University of Puerto Rico, 2002.

Rodríguez-Inoa, E.A. "Fideicomiso de Conservación de Puerto Rico: modelo alternativo para proteger los recursos naturales." MA thesis, University of Puerto Rico, 2011.

Sachs, J. D., and A. Warner. "Economic Reform and the Process of Global Integration." *Brookings Papers on Economic Activity* 1 (1995): 1–118.

Sanna-Randaccio, F. and R. Sestini. "The Impact of Unilateral Climate Policy with Endogenous Plant Location and Market Size Asymmetry." *Review of International Economics* 20 (2012): 439–656.

Sardosky, P. "Renewable Energy Consumption, CO2 Emissions and Oil Prices in the G7 Countries." *Energy Economics* 31, no. 1 (2009): 456–462.

Segarra-Alméstica, E.V. "What happened to the distribution of income in Puerto Rico during the last three decades of the XX century? A statistical point of view." *Ensayos y Monografías* no. 129, Unidad de Investigaciones Económicas, Departamento de Economía, Universidad de Puerto Rico, 2006.

Seguinot-Barbosa, J. *Islas en extinción: el impacto ambiental en las islas de Puerto Rico.* Ediciones SM, 2011.

Sotomayor, O. "Development and Income Distribution: The case of Puerto Rico." *World Development* 32, no. 8 (2004): 1395–1406.

Sturgeon, T. J. *The Automotive Industry in Vietnam: Prospects for Development in a Globalizing Economy Appendix IV of the Industrial Competitiveness Review Report prepared for: Development Strategy Institute Ministry of Planning and Investment Vietnam, and Medium-Term Industrial Strategy Project.* Report. United Nations Industrial Development Organization Vietnam. 1998.

Suárez, S. L. "Lessons Learned: Explaining the Political Behavior of Business." *Polity* 31, no. 1 (1998): 161–186. doi:10.2307/3235371

Svedberg, P. "Colonial Enforcement of Foreign Direct Investment." *The Manchester School* 49, no. 1 (1981): 21–38.

Tientenberg, T. H. "Reflections-Carbon Pricing in Practice." *Review of Environmental Economics and Policy* 7, no. 2 (2013): 313–329.

Tolentino, P. E. *Multinational Corporations: Emergence and Evolution.* London, UK: Routledge, 2000.

U.S. Barriers toTrade and Investment Barriers Report 2015. Report. Brussels: European Commission, 2015.

U.S.A. U.S. Department of Commerce. International Trade Administration. *Guide to the Caribbean Basin Initiative.* 2000 ed. Washington, DC: ITA, 2000. November 2000. http://www.ita.doc.gov/media/Publications/pdf/cbi2000.pdf (accessed February 13, 2017).

UNCTAD (2005) "Methodologies, classifications, quantification and development impacts of non-tariff barriers" TD/B/COM.1/EM.27/2 Available http://unctad.org/en/Docs/c1em27d2_en.pdf

———. (2007) "Market access, market entry and competitiveness" TD/B/COM.1/83 Available http://unctad.org/en/Docs/c1d83_en.pdf

———. (2012) "Evolution of non-tariff measures: Emerging cases from selected developing countries" *Policy Issues in International Trade and Commodities.* Study Series No. 52. http://unctad.org/en/PublicationsLibrary/itcdtab53_en.pdfhttp://unctad.org/en/PublicationsLibrary/itcdtab53_en.pdf (accessed 17 February, 2017).

———. (2014) "Local content requirements and the green economy." UNCTAD-DITCTED20137, United Nations. unctad.orgenPublicationsLibraryditcted2013d7_en.pdf (accessed 17 February, 2017).

UNIDO (1986) "Industrial policy and the developing countries: An analysis of local content regulations." UNIDO/IS; 606.

———. (2011a) "The Vietnam industrial investment report: Understanding the impact of foreign direct investment on industrial development." http://www.unido.org/fileadmin/user_media/Publications/Pub_free/VIIR%20print.pdf (accessed 17 February, 2017).

———. (2011b) "Africa investor report: Towards evidence-based investment promotion strategies." http://www.unido.org/fileadmin/user_media/ Publications/Pub_free/AIS_Report_A4.pdf (accessed 17 February, 2017).

USITC (2013) "Effects of significant US import restraints." Publication 4440. Investigation number 332–325.

USTR (2013) "Tenth report to Congress on the operation of the Caribbean Basin Economic Recovery Act." *Office of the United States Trade Representative.* http://www.ustr.gov/sites/default/files/CBERA%20Report%20Final.pdf (accessed 17 February, 2017).

———. (2015) "2015 National Trade Estimates Report on Foreign Trade Barrier." *United States Trade Representative*, March 2015.

Vega-Rosado, L.L. "The International Competitiveness of Puerto Rico using the Porter's Model" *Journal of Global Competitiveness* 14, no. 2 (2006): 95–111.

Venator-Santiago, C.R. *Puerto Rico and the Origins of U.S. Global Empire.* Routledge Publishers, 2015.

Vinokurov, E., Balas, P., Emerson, M., Havlik, P., Vladimir, P., Rovenskaya, E., Stepanova, A., Kofner, J., and P. Kabat "Non-tariff barriers and technical regulations" IIASA project *Challenges and Opportunities of Economic Integration within a Wider European and Eurasian Space.* Workshop Report. (2016) http://pure.iiasa.ac.at/13968/1/Non-tariff%20barriers%20and%20technical%20regulations.pdf (accessed 17 February, 2017).

Wacziarg, R. and K. H. Welch. "Trade Liberalization and Growth: New evidence." *The World Bank Economic Review* 22, no. 2 (2008): 187–231.

Walker, T. C. (1995) Environmental markets: Puerto Rico. Project commissioned by the Government of Puerto Rico.

Walter, I. "Non-Tariff and Free-Trade Area Option." *PLS Quarterly Review* 22, no. 88 (1969): 16–45.

Wildasin, D. E. "Nash Equilibria in Models of Fiscal Competition." *Journal of Public Economics* 35, no. 2 (1988): 229–240.

Zayas-Oliveras, H. "Análisis de veinte años en la lucha ambiental de Puerto Rico del 1980 al 2000." MA thesis, Inter-American University, Puerto Rico, 2006.

Index

Page references for figures and tables are italicized.

About the Author

Luis Gautier is an assistant professor of economics at the University of Texas at Tyler. His research interests include applied microeconomics, environmental economics, and issues of development in the Caribbean Basin. He has published in reputable academic journals such as *Resource and Energy Economics, Journal of Public Economic Theory*, and *Environment and Development Economics*. Dr. Gautier graduated from the University of Puerto Rico, Río Piedras Campus, with a BS in economics, and his graduate work includes an MSc in economics from the University of Warwick and an MA in Political Economy from the University of Essex in the United Kingdom, as well as a PhD in economics from Southern Illinois University, Carbondale, USA.

Lightning Source UK Ltd.
Milton Keynes UK
UKOW04n0800021217

313701UK00001BA/38/P

9 781498 556835